Rebecca Ramus

God Is

John Bisagno

This book is designed for your personal reading pleasure and profit. It is also designed for group study. A Leader's Guide with helps and hints for teachers and with visual aids (Victor Multiuse Transparency Masters) is available from your local bookstore or from the publisher.

VICTOR

BOOKS a division of SP Publications, Inc.
WHEATON, ILLINOIS 60187

Offices also in
Whitby, Ontario, Canada
Amersham-on-the-Hill, Bucks, England

All Scripture quotations are from the *King James Bible.*

Recommended Dewey Decimal Classification: 231.4
  Suggested Subject Heading: ATTRIBUTES OF GOD

Library of Congress Catalog Card Number: 83-060824
ISBN: 0-88207-345-1

VICTOR BOOKS
A division of SP Publications, Inc.
P.O. Box 1825 • Wheaton, Illinois 60187

CONTENTS

Preface

God. That three-letter word conjures up all sorts of images to modern man. To many, the word represents Someone unknown. To some, it is a word to be feared. But to those of us who know God intimately, the name brings to mind thoughts of love, kindness, mercy, and an ever-present Friend.

God is not something or someone in the far distance of outer space. He is not something to fear, unless we turn away from Him.

God has placed within the human personality the capacity to know Him. We can have fellowship with God. He is not just the Ruler of heaven and earth, but He is also as close as our own hearts. We can know God better than we know our best friends.

"How?" some may ask. Volition, or the capacity to choose fellowship with God, is that divine gift to the human race which sets us apart and above all other created beings. We can know God because God wants us to know Him. To approach Him, to know Him, to experience Him, to love Him, is the greatest gift that God has given to mankind.

Yet, though we may know God in Jesus Christ, we will never know Him fully in this life. God is much greater than we can ever comprehend in our present form and with our present minds. This doesn't mean we should give up because we cannot know Him completely. Quite the contrary. Just to know a little about God is to comprehend great mysteries and to obtain abundant knowledge.

One truth which stands out in the Bible is that the redeemed of the Lord may continually know Him better. We are expected to grow in grace and knowledge and in our understanding of God. We may never know all there is to know about God, but we can learn much as we draw closer to Him and to His Word, our Bible, and to His people, the church.

It is said that the Old Testament translators upon writing the word for "God" would pick up a new quill before penning the word and burn it afterward. So awed were they of the greatness of God that they dared not even use the same pen to write His name that penned any other truth.

To the ancient Hebrews, knowing the name of God—Yahweh—meant knowing something very important and very priceless.

With reverence, yet with courage, let us study in the next 10 chapters what God is like. There is so much about Him to learn. Let us therefore look at the attributes of God to see what we can learn about the One whose we are and whom we serve.

God Is
Sovereign
1

[handwritten margin note: - above or superior to all others - supreme in power, rank, authority -]

Know ye that the Lord, He is God. It is He that hath made us, and not we ourselves. We are His people, and the sheep of His pasture.   *Psalm 100:3*

Believing simultaneously in the sovereignty of God and in the freedom of man seems contradictory. Many people ask, "How can God be a Sovereign and absolute Ruler, and at the same time allow His supreme creation, man, to be free to choose his own destiny?"

Even among some Christian theologians, debates go on over how God, who lives and reigns with total power and dominion over the universe, can tolerate or allow people to have free wills.

The answer to this dilemma is actually quite simple. The fact that everyone has a free will is perhaps the ultimate testimony to the sovereignty of the loving, wise, and all-knowing God. God is so secure, so powerful, and so much in control that He is able to allow people to choose for themselves which destinies they will follow. And because people are free, they

7

have the capacity to accept or reject union with God.

We should not view the biblical doctrines of human free will and the sovereignty of God as contradictory. We should view them as mutually compatible, for that is what they are.

One must adequately understand the nature of God before he can find the key to unlock the mysterious connection between God's sovereignty and people's free will. God ultimately expressed His sovereignty when He allowed people to make their own choices. Endowing people with volition is in reality an act of God's sovereignty.

People have the choice of whether to accept or reject this sovereign God. The decision is not God's, but ours. Our highest and greatest use of this freedom, then, is to choose to acknowledge and experience the sovereignty of God in our lives.

The opposite is also true: people's lowest and poorest use of their freedom is to turn and choose to ignore and run away from the sovereignty of God in their lives.

The saddest and most miserable people in the world are those who rebel totally against this sovereign God. But one must remember that they have chosen this state of rebellion for their own lives. God did not will it for them. They willed it for themselves. God has given all of us the right to choose. The choice is ours. God loves us enough to let us make this decision about our own lives.

When a person's will is in voluntary submission to his Creator, the result is a life lived in harmony with God's sovereignty. No two doctrines are more mutually compatible than those of God's sovereignty and man's free will.

God's Sovereign Nature

So what does it mean to speak of the sovereign nature of God? And what kind of Sovereign is He? Is He like the sovereigns of the world, who rule by force and often with total lack of empathy for their subjects?

The writer of Psalm 100 said this about God: "It is He that hath made us, and not we ourselves." The author of Genesis expressed this same idea: God is our Creator. He made the whole universe. "In the beginning, God created the heaven and the earth" (Gen. 1:1).

But more than that, "God is God." No human being can ever be God, for God is greater than His creation. He who creates is greater that he who is created.

Yet, how often do human beings try to take this God-role upon themselves? Yes, in a way we all want to be God! We may not express it directly, but we all want to be in control of our lives and in control of the world around us. Eventually, each person must answer the question, "Who is going to rule my life? God or me?"

It was Lucifer's answer to this question which initially unbalanced the universe and introduced sin into God's perfect Creation. Before God created our world Lucifer, the archangel, declared, "I will exalt my throne above the stars of God" (Isa. 14:13). In Eden Lucifer, who appears to have become Satan, promised Eve and Adam, "Ye shall be as gods" (Gen. 3:5).

Since this initial declaration of war on the right of the sovereign God to rule, all of history has been moving toward a final Armageddon resolution of the question, "Is God going to be God or isn't He?"

God Is in Control

God is sovereign because He is the One who is ultimately in control of His creation. He has given man the freedom to choose right or wrong, good or evil, God or Satan, heaven or hell. God will not make these choices for us. He lets us make them ourselves. But He has also determined what the consequences of our choices will be.

There is another way to view the sovereignty of God: nothing happens until it is filtered through God's permissive will.

God does not will that certain things will happen; He permits them to happen. He gives people the choice of whether to choose right or wrong. He does not will that anyone choose evil. But when someone chooses wrong, God permits him to make that choice.

A psalmist said, "The earth is the Lord's, and the fullness thereof" (Ps. 24:1). The Bible also says, "All things were created by Him, and for Him, and . . . by Him all things consist" (Col. 1:16-17).

God doesn't change His mind. He doesn't ask advice. He never makes a mistake. He is sovereign, irrepressible, unconquerable, immutable, loving, and the eternal God of grace. Nothing happens without His permission. He gave that permission when He gave us our freedom.

Man's Rebellion

Robert Browning, a famous poet, once put this comment into the mouth of one of his creations, Little Pippa: "God's in His heaven—all's right with the world!"

That statement makes beautiful poetry but it is poor theology. True, God is in His heaven. And He is also in His creation. He is both transcendent and immanent. He is in heaven and in Houston, Dallas, New York City, Paris, London, Singapore, Moscow, and every place on earth. God is everywhere.

But one only has to see today's newspaper headlines or watch the news on TV to see that all's *not* right with the world. People are free to choose what their own destinies will be, and often their choices are wrong. Beneath God's sovereignty people still struggle over choices. Often they fail.

When someone asks about the nature of God, he is really asking, "What right does God have over the earth and over my life?" Every century and almost every decade this century, we have seen a new philosophy emerge, designed to try to overthrow the sovereignty of God.

What used to be the largest church in Russia has been converted into a museum of space exploration. The altar has been replaced with pictures of the first two Russian cosmonauts to fly into space. Beneath their pictures are their famous words: "We have searched the heavens, and we did not find God." Communism says, "God does not exist. We ourselves are God."

The Communists are not alone in this attitude. They have many partners in this world. One reason the Nazis hated the Jews so much was that the Jews represented God to them. The Bible—including its writers, its holidays, its prophets, its Messiah—were Jewish. All people who have hated God through the centuries have somehow found it in their hearts to hate the Jewish people. This sad fact is still true in our world today.

Communism and Nazism have their counterparts in other contemporary philosophies. Atheism, materialism, playboyism, secularism—they all make their subtle claims to being the saviors of the world. According to these philosophies, God is unnecessary and totally useless. Each philosophy teaches that a person can function as his own god, can satisfy his own deep inner longings, and can help create a world that does not need divine control or intervention.

Even teachings in certain segments of the church today subtly lead people in the same direction as these anti-God philosophies. One of these teachings is known as "positive affirmation." This so-called theology teaches that Christians can pray a blessing of protection on their homes, their children, and on everything in their physical world, so that no ill effect will ever befall them or theirs. According to this doctrine, the right kind of prayer offers protection from flat tires, illness, hurricanes, job layoffs, etc. This doctrine claims that by "positive affirmation," or "positive confession," they can create perfect environments for themselves and their families.

This teaching, though wrapped in Christian language and supposedly drawn from the Bible, contradicts God's Word.

The Scriptures plainly teach that God permits, and even sends, problems and negative circumstances into our lives to chastise us, to correct us, and to allow His grace to be revealed through us. "Positive affirmation" subtly teaches that we can become like God, by making a request through a simple prayer. Following this idea to its conclusion, God becomes our Servant— the Big Daddy in the sky, who jumps at our beck and call. Instead of teaching that God is sovereign, "positive affirmation" teaches that God can become exactly what we want Him to be—our Sugar Daddy who races about meeting our every request and enacting our every whim. In reality, we Christians are invited to let our requests be made known to God—not our demands!

How tragic when Christians view God as Big Daddy in the sky instead of their sovereign Lord and Master. God is God. He is not our personal slave who reacts to our every demand. Those who teach "positive affirmation" say that when we pray "in His name" and "in His will," God builds a "heavenly protection around people who are the victims of partial knowledge."

These proponents make ridiculous demands, inferring that they know better how to order their lives than God does. This is ludicrous! God is God. It is far better to pray, "Thy will be done" than to demand that God become our cosmic Slave.

God must remain God if He is to be our God and we are to remain His people. Never will we become gods and God become our creation. When we pray, "Thy will be done," we do not know God's perfect will for our lives or for the lives of those for whom we pray. The measure of authenticity of any Christian doctrine ought to be a yes answer to each of these questions: "Does the doctrine glorify Jesus Christ? Is Jesus Lord? Is God in control? Is God our sovereign Lord?" If the answer to any of these queries is no, then that doctrine, regardless of how wonderful it sounds, is not of God.

God's Greatness

Any study of God's sovereignty must enlarge our understanding of God's greatness. The children's prayer at dinnertime—"God is great. God is good. Let us thank Him for our food"—expresses this concept so simply and yet so well. Indeed, God is great. He created our world with a pronouncement from heaven. He can destroy it with a wave of His hand. Before Him, the nations are like a drop in the bucket, or like a pebble on the beach. It is God who spoke and thus created the world. And it is He who is "upholding all things by the Word of His power" (Heb. 1:3).

In his letter to the great Dutch scholar Erasmus, Martin Luther said, "Your thoughts of God are too human." Many Christian songs and little sermonettes are nothing more than theological treatises which open the door to the basis of all doctrinal error—the tendency to humanize God and deify man.

Yes, we must admit that sometimes the Bible expresses God in human terms. Theologians have a fancy word for this—they call it anthropomorphism. Human terms were used to convey certain truths about God. For instance, our Lord taught us to think in terms of God as "our Father which art in heaven." But then He immediately added, "Hallowed be Thy name" (Matt. 6:9). When we encounter these anthropomorphic terms, we must be cautious. Familiarity must not breed contempt. Nothing opens the door more quickly to untruth, cultism, and heresy than does the subtle teaching that God is no more than a human being, and that man is really a god. Some religions teach that since God Himself "began as a man and evolved," we too may someday evolve into what God is now. That is wrong! We can never become sovereign gods. Only God is sovereign. And God was never a mere human creature, either. God existed before His Creation. God has no beginning and no ending. Jesus was both divine and human.

He had God for His Father and Mary for His mother.

In heaven, in our glorified state, we shall be like God and see Him as He is. We shall know as He knows, love as He loves, and understand fully.

But we will still be God's creatures. Glorified? Yes. Divine? No. We shall remain the products of God's handiwork, though remade into the image of His Son, Jesus Christ. God will still be God. We will still be His subjects. We will worship Him and serve Him forever.

Man's Obedience

Because God is sovereign, He has the right to exercise control over our lives. It is a great mistake to teach or imply that man is motivated to serve God because of emotional or sentimental reasons alone rather than because God asks our obedience. The more we obey God, the more we discover that He has our best interests at heart. And the more we learn to trust God, the more we love Him. The initial basis of our response to God is our obedience to His sovereignty—to His right to control our lives.

The Lord says, "These things hast thou done, and I kept silence; thou thoughtest that I was altogether such an one as thyself; but I will reprove thee, and set them in order before thine eyes. Now consider this, ye that forget God, lest I tear you in pieces, and there be none to deliver. Whoso offereth praise glorifieth Me; and to him that ordereth his conversation aright will I show the salvation of God" (Ps. 50:21-23).

Once we settle that God is God, then we resolve that He should be served. In serving Him, we learn that He is good. Because He is good, we come to love Him. Love is the result of our knowing and trusting God. Virtues result from obeying God. Obeying God as the sovereign One, who rules our lives, is the basis of all service and of all blessing.

God's Sovereign Control

The sovereigns of earth may try to order God's overthrow through their power, but they will never succeed. It can't be done. God's Son, who is the same yesterday, today, and forever (Heb. 13:8), is quietly about the work of building His kingdom on schedule, in an orderly way, just as He has always done. Far beyond the power of man, the sovereign God has everything in His control. At His bidding the worlds were flung into space and the stars placed in their paths. At His bidding the earth brought forth her fruit in due season, animals reproduced, and people multiplied. At His bidding fire fell from heaven, locusts covered the earth, the death angel killed Egypt's first-born, and the earth swallowed thousands as rebels were judged in the wilderness. At His bidding manna fell from heaven, the sea parted, and Joshua commanded the sun to stand still. At His bidding an ax head floated, lions' mouths closed, and the fires of a pagan furnace cooled.

Who is man that he thinks he can judge God? And who is man that he thinks he can upstage and outdistance God? The sovereign God created this world. The sovereign God created people. The sovereign God gave us our freedom. The sovereign God lets us exercise our freedom. And in the end, the sovereign God will judge our use of that freedom.

Despite all the theories, philosophies, and theologies that man can produce, God is still Sovereign of the universe, of all creation.

The sovereignty of God is a doctrine hated by the world. People will allow God to shower them with blessings, uphold the earth in His right hand, light the lamp of heaven, and rule the restless waves of the sea. Yet many gnash their teeth and proclaim God dethroned when He insists on the right to rule their hearts. The heathen make gods of wood and stone. The cultured make gods of sex, materialism, and pleasure. But such gods, whose wills can be resisted by their creators, are no gods at all. The Lord is the only sovereign God. In sickness and health, inflation and depression, war and peace, life and death, God is still in control of this world. He is sovereign.

If all the rulers of this world were today to declare war against Almighty God, it would have less effect on Him than does the churning of the Mediterranean on the mighty Rock of Gibraltar. All God sets out to do, He does. All He has ever been, He is. His will cannot be frustrated. His church cannot be crushed. His Word cannot pass away. His promises cannot fail. His plans cannot be thwarted. His power cannot be resisted.

Why don't people understand God's sovereignty? This perplexing question has troubled generation after generation of both Jews and Christians. A psalmist wrote, "Why do the heathen rage, and the people imagine a vain thing? The kings of the earth set themselves, and the rulers take counsel together, against the Lord, and against His annointed, saying, 'Let us break their bands asunder, and cast away their cords from us.' He that sitteth in the heavens shall laugh; the Lord shall have them in derision" (Ps. 2:1-4).

And again the Bible says, "Jehoshaphat stood in the congregation of Judah and Jerusalem, in the house of the Lord, before the new court, and said, 'O Lord God of our fathers, art not Thou God in heaven? And rulest not Thou over all the kingdoms of the heathen? And in Thine hand is there not power and might, so that none is able to withstand Thee?'" (2 Chron. 20:5-6)

When the sands of time have been washed upon the shores of eternity, Jesus Christ will be King of kings and Lord of lords, and there will be peace in the universe through Him, the sovereign Lord and Master of the universe.

Man's Humble Response

Such unusurpable power in the hands of an earthly potentate would be devastating. No man could be trusted with such authority. But wonder of wonders: He who is all authority and all power knows me and loves me. The great Creator became our Saviour and died on an old rugged cross for even us. This doctrine should constrain our deepest fidelity and devote us to exercise our wills in harmony with His. Just imagine! He who created us, who could so easily damn and destroy us, is the very One who cherishes us so much that He gave Himself for us. He is our Sovereign.

2
God Is
Loving

As Moses lifted up the serpent in the wilderness, even so must the Son of man be lifted up; that whosoever believeth in Him should not perish, but have eternal life. For God so loved the world, that He gave His only begotten Son, that whosoever believeth in Him should not perish, but have everlasting life. For God sent not His Son into the world to condemn the world; but that the world through Him might be saved. He that believeth on Him is not condemned; but he that believeth not is condemned already, because he hath not believed in the name of the only begotten Son of God.   John 3:14-18

God is love. These three little words form a far-reaching and powerful, yet simple, statement about our God. All the characteristics of God must be understood in the context of these three tiny words. The testimony that "God is love" forms the key that unlocks many mysteries about God.

If we fail to understand that God is a God of love, we fail to grasp the full meaning of His personality. Without a doctrine of God's love, we are lost in our quest to understand the full dimensions of God's grandeur, His sovereignty, His immutability, His glory, and His majesty. The irrepressible power of God is cast in the characteristic of love. In His sovereignty, God hates sin, judges sin, and punishes sinners. Were it not for God's love, His sovereignty would demand that every human being be crushed, judged, damned, and destroyed the minute he sins.

But when we discuss the love of God, we must be careful to keep it in the proper perspective. God's love cannot be viewed apart from His other traits. Love is like the glue that binds together the other personality characteristics of God and gives them a sharper, clearer meaning and focus. Yet, love is a separate quality, though at the same time it is the door to understanding His other characteristics.

The love of God is not some cheap potion that negates all His other qualities. When we fail to understand that God is a God of love, we miss an essential element in His personality. When we raise love to the height of being God's only characteristic, we miss the breadth and width of His personality. Love is a key element in understanding God, but it is not the only ingredient, as many would have us believe.

Who Is God?

Ask 10 Christians gathered in a Sunday School class this question: What is God like? At least 8, and maybe all 10, will answer that God is a God of love. Love is a well-known attribute of God. But ask 10 theologians and philosophers a similar question: Who is God? The answers will probably not be so simple. Some may echo the popular theological expression that "God is the ground of our being." Others may quote Sigmund Freud and say that God is the creation of man's deepest needs and desires. One might even quote Ludwig Feuerbach and say that God is the projection of what we wish our own earthly fathers had been like. Others would describe God as "the good old man upstairs." Still others would ask, "Which god are we talking about—the god of the Muslims, the God of the Jews, the God of the Christians, or one of the various gods of the Hindus?" To many in this world, our God is wrongly viewed as just one deity among many others.

We cannot understand who God is without understanding what God is like. And we cannot understand what God is like without understanding the characteristics of God, especially the love of God.

Let us, then, explore further this important question: Who is God? And let us turn to our primary source for answering this question: our Bible. We must remember that we cannot understand God apart from the Bible, for it is the record of God's revelation of Himself to man. Philosophers and theologians try to understand God by searching their own minds for ideas. But the best guide for understanding God is His Word, both the Old and New Testaments. The Bible gives us three answers to the question, "Who is God?"

will never reveal God

First, the Bible says that "God is a spirit, and they that worship Him must worship Him in spirit and in truth" (John 4:24). The word "a" is not in the Greek text, so the passage should be rendered, "God is spirit." This means that God is not a physical, created being. God is not limited by a physical body. He is not visible to us. He may not be touched, controlled, bottled up, handled, or contained. God is omnipresent, omniscient, and omnipotent: He is everywhere at once, knows everything at once, and controls everything at once. When we say we hear the voice of God in our lives, we do not mean that we hear Him speaking in audible terms. God is totally spirit. He speaks only by His holy tug on our hearts. Our spiritual ears must be attuned in order to hear His voice.

Second, the Bible says, "God is light, and in Him is no darkness at all" (1 John 1:5). Satan is master of the kingdom of evil and darkness. Christ is Lord of the kingdom of holiness and light. When we come to Christ, we come to the One who is "the Light of the world" and "the true Light which lighteth every man that cometh into the world" (John 1:9).

Third, "God is love" (1 John 4:8). This does not mean that God is an abstraction, such as envy or persuasion, pity or success. It means that the totality of all that God is and does is love. The fruit of the Spirit is love (Gal. 5:22). The result of having God in one's life is a loving disposition. The love mentioned in this verse is different from the common understanding of love in our society. This love is a moving, powerful force that reaches out with compassion, understanding, empathy, and a desire to see that which is loved attain its full potential in life.

These three characteristics—spirit, light, and love—answer the question, "Who is God?" These three attributes of God provide the basis for our doctrine of God. They make a complete statement about Him.

God is spirit; God is light; God is love. Fully one-third of the nature of God is biblically described in terms of love. God's love, then, must be seen as an expression of His nature, which is itself love.

Because God is love, He loves. His sovereignty cannot be contained; neither can His love. His love must be expressed. And it is. The Bible says, "While we were yet sinners, Christ died for us" (Rom. 5:8). Christ is the ultimate expression of God's love for us. "In this was manifested the love of God toward us, because that God sent His only begotten Son into the world, that we might live through Him" (1 John 4:9).

We may not respond positively to God's love for us. We may reject and even disdain His love. But that does not mean He does not love us. He loves us nonetheless. Even when God's sovereign nature consigns an unpenitent sinner to eternal damnation, God's loving nature continues to reach out to that same sinner, in sorrow and in pity.

Love Is Something You Do

The love of God is not something merely spoken or sung. Yes, we can speak about this love. We can even sing beautiful, glorious hymns about it. But God's love is something that must be experienced. It is available to every person, regardless of how deeply one is mired in sin.

The love of God is something that must happen. It must happen deep inside our hearts. It must be experienced in the depths of our very beings. It is not enough to know that Jesus Christ died on the cross for you and for me—that a carpenter from Nazareth was nailed to two pieces of wood on the city garbage dump 2,000 years ago. Those are historical facts. These facts mean little more than do other histories, such as those of the Crusades or the battle of Waterloo. It is only when the death and resurrection of Jesus are experienced deep inside our souls that we understand them fully. The death of Jesus Christ on the cross is much more than a historical fact. It means much more to you and me than the Crusades or the battle of Waterloo—but only if we let it.

The death of Jesus Christ on the cross of Calvary was God's greatest expression of His love reaching out to us. On the cross, God reached out to us, to touch us and to save us.

It is possible for us to miss this expression. We miss it when we fail to realize what the cross means. It is a tragedy when we fail to open our hearts and to experience this love that God extends to us. If we refuse to open ourselves to God, we will never truly know what the love of God is all about. It is not enough to merely say, "God is love." We must experience it so we can say, "We know 'God is love' because we feel His love deep within us."

How can one describe the beauty of a sunset to a blind person? Or the gorgeous strains of a symphony to one who is deaf? Or the succulent flavor of a prime piece of meat to one who has no sense of taste? These things must be experienced.

So must the love of God be felt in our hearts. It is one thing to know that God is love. It is another to experience this love in our own lives.

Love Is Not Something We Can Earn

The love of God is not something we can earn. We cannot deserve it by working for it. We cannot beg for it. We cannot bargain for it. We can only experience it. The Bible says, "Herein is love, not that we loved God, but that He loved us, and sent His Son to be the propitiation for our sins" (1 John 4:10).

God did not send Jesus to die for our sins because *we* loved *Him* so much that He wanted to do something for us. God sent Jesus to us because *He* loved *us* so much that He wanted to do this for us.

God loves us, sinners that we are. We cannot clean ourselves up to make ourselves worthy of being loved by God. Christ died for sinners. God loved the world as no human has ever loved another. Jesus Christ, the only begotten Son of God, hung on the cross because God loves you and me.

Some people say to me, "I'm too bad to be saved. I'm too mean to be a Christian. I've got too many sins to be converted."

I say to them, "That's why God wants you to be converted. That's why you need to be saved." Our Lord Jesus Christ said, "I came not to call the righteous, but sinners to repentance" (Luke 5:32). Confessing that we are sinners is what it means to open our hearts up to God. We are saved not because we are good, but because God is good and loving, and He accepts us even though we are sinful.

God's love cannot be earned. We cannot achieve it. We can do nothing to merit it. The Bible says, "For by grace are ye saved through faith, and that not of yourselves; it is the gift of God; not of works, lest any man should boast" (Eph. 2:8-9). If you have to work to obtain something, it is no longer a gift. God's grace is not deserved. God was in Christ doing for sinners not only what we do not deserve and cannot earn, but also doing what we cannot do for ourselves.

You may say, "Tomorrow I'll quit my sins. Tomorrow I'll become good enough. Tomorrow I'll clean myself up." But tomorrow will never come. Even if you could—which you can't—get to the place where you never sin, you could still not approach God and say, "Now I'm good enough. Now I'm ready to be saved."

God would look at you and say: "Go back and sit down. I can't save you. 'They that are whole need not a physician' (Luke 5:31). Those who think they are all right do not need My services. The self-righteous do not need Me. If you are well, you don't need a spiritual doctor. For people who come to Me come as they are—sinful and guilt-ridden."

On the cross Jesus, who had never known sin, who had never sinned, became sin for you and for me. In the six hours that He hung on the cross—an awesome experience which this world will never fully comprehend—Jesus became sin. That's why the Bible says, "As Moses lifted up the serpent in the wilderness, even so must the Son of man [Christ] be lifted up" (John 3:14). Why a serpent? Why not a lily, a symbol of something beautiful? Because Christ became sin. That was my sin hanging on the cross. That was your sin hanging on the cross. Jesus became sin so that God could pour out His wrath and His judgment of sin through Christ. The Bible says, "Surely He hath borne our griefs, and carried our sorrows; yet we did esteem Him stricken, smitten of God, and afflicted. But He was wounded for our transgressions, He was bruised for our iniquities" (Isa. 53:4-5). God put His judgment on my sins, on the body of His own Son, on the cross. That's what we mean when we sing, "Jesus paid it all; all to Him I owe. Sin had left a crimson stain; He washed it white as snow."

Some popular stories attempt to tell what it was like for God to empty Himself for us on the cross. None tell of the incarnation as well as the Bible does, but they help put theological thoughts into contemporary language.

For example, there's the story of the sailor who came to a ship's captain and said, "Sir, my little dog has fallen overboard. Will you stop this ship so that I might rescue him?"

The captain responded, "Son, this ship does not stop for a dog."

The young man replied, "Sir, if it were a person, would you stop?"

The captain answered, "We would."

Immediately the sailor jumped overboard. He rescued his dog and waited for the captain to turn the ship around and rescue both of them.

In this story, the sailor took on himself the plight of the dog. He identified with his pet. Jesus Christ was like this young man, but in a much greater way. He too did not just stand on the sidelines and give advice. He became our sin.

The late Louis Cassels, former religion editor of United Press International, told another story that illustrates what it meant for Jesus to become our sin for us. Cassels told about a man watching from the warmth of his house while a flock of birds circled outside in a snowstorm. The man wanted to help the birds and eventually went outside to open his barn door, hoping the birds would find shelter inside the barn. But the birds were afraid and refused to enter. The man went back to his house and watched tearfully as the birds continued to circle aimlessly. As he watched, the man thought, "If only I could become a bird like those that are outside, then I could fly out to meet them and lead them inside my barn to safety and warmth."

The man in this story did not have the power that God has. God saw humanity wandering in its sin. He not only *wanted* to do something for us; He *did*. In Jesus Christ, God became a Man to lead us out of our sin. Jesus became our sin for us.

A Chinese man who was saved years ago came to America to give his testimony. He told it like this: "I had walked through the road of life and had fallen into a great ditch of sin. Muhammad came along and said, 'You're not really in that ditch; you just think you are there.' Buddha came along and said to me, 'Here are seven steps by which you can get out of that ditch. If you will climb and struggle, you will come out.' I strove, but I could not get out. Then Confucius came by and said, 'Here are 10 steps of self-attainment, by which you can get out of that ditch. If you can come half of the way, I'll come the other half, and take you out.' But struggle as I would, I still was in my pit of sin, hopeless and helpless.

"Then one day, the Nazarene came by. Jesus saw my condition. Without a word of advice, He stripped Himself of His regal robes and stepped to the earth through the womb of the Virgin. He who had never sinned, became sin for me. He got down in the ditch, into the muck and the mud, into the sin, and lifted me up. Thank God, what I could not do for myself, Christ did for me."

A favorite Gospel song beautifully expresses this same idea:

> In loving-kindness Jesus came,
> My soul in mercy to reclaim.
> And from the depths of sin and shame
> Through grace He lifted me.
> From sinking sand He lifted me;
> With tender hand He lifted me.
> From shades of night to plains of light;
> Oh, praise His name, He lifted me!
> —Charles H. Gabriel

We cannot lift ourselves from the sin-filled ditch of our lives. The Chinese man couldn't lift himself out of that ditch. You cannot lift yourself out of it either. Jesus didn't tell the man how to climb out. He didn't advise him. He didn't sit on the edge and philosophize about his predicament. Jesus didn't offer a number of theories for the man to contemplate. Jesus simply got into the ditch with the man and lifted him out into safety.

These three stories all illustrate the nature of God's love. You cannot struggle and improve yourself until you receive God's love. You can only open your heart to Jesus and let Him do in and through you what you can never do for yourself.

God's Love Is Inexhaustible
The love of God is inexhaustible. We must tell the world that there is still room at the foot of the cross for every person who wants to be there. Think of it like this: "For God so loved the world"—so loved you, that He gave His only begotten Son, that if you will believe on Him, you will not perish, but *have* everlasting life (John 3:16).

It takes no more of the blood of Christ to cleanse the most hardened sinner than it does to forgive the smallest child. If I were the only sinner in all the world, Jesus Christ would have still cared enough for me that He would have come from heaven's glory and died on the cross for me. But, though He would have come for only one sinner, the blood that flowed from His wounds is strong and effective and powerful enough to cleanse all the vilest sinners who come to Him.

God's Love Is Also Inevitable
The love of God is also inevitable. This means that it simply had to be. The Bible says that God is love. As a loving God, He simply could not stand by and watch humanity continue forever lost and separated in spiritual death. God's great heart was moved with compassion for us. He became the divine Initiator, the great Originator. He brought about the means for our salvation.

The Bible says, "The wages of sin is death" (Rom. 6:23). Dead people cannot produce any goodness and life that seeks after God, any more than dead wood can produce leaves and flowers. Because we couldn't save ourselves, God in Christ came seeking us. He loved you and me so much that His Son died on the cross for us. If I open my heart and experience His love, I am pardoned; I am a child of God, justified before my heavenly Father, and rightly related to God by faith in Jesus Christ. In gratitude I give Him my life and love in return.

Some years ago a preacher in Boston had an experience which illustrates the love that God has for us. As Dr. A. J. Gordon came out of his church one morning, a little boy stood in the alley with a cage. In the cage were some small field birds—wrens and sparrows.

Gordon asked, "Son, what are you going to do with your birds?"

The freckle-faced boy said, "Look here, mister," as he pulled and tugged on one of their wings. "I like to make them scream. I'm going to torture them and have some fun, and then I'm going to feed them to the cats."

Gordon instantly replied, "Son, I'd like to have those birds."

The boy said, "Mister, you don't really want them. They ain't good for nothing."

The wise minister said, "Well, son, I was a boy like you once. I know these birds' names. I recognize their voices and the color of their feathers. I'd love to have them."

The boy was also an enterprising businessman. "Mister, you'll have to pay for them," he said.

"How much?" Gordon asked.

"You wouldn't pay it," the boy said.

"I'll pay anything you ask," said the minister.

"Really?" The boy's eyes lit up. And as though he were asking for the world, the boy said, "Five whole dollars."

"Well," said Gordon, "that isn't too bad." He reached into

his pocket and paid the price and took the birds.

As the boy went his way, Gordon decided he must do something with the birds. So he opened the door of the cage to let them fly away. Afraid, the birds just huddled in the cage and refused to move. Gordon then nudged one of them and it finally flew away, circling overhead and chirping as if to say, "I'm free. I'm free!" Then the other birds followed, one after the other.

Gordon said this experience reminded him of a Chinese legend which goes this way:

One day Jesus was walking across heaven. He came up to Satan who had a cage full of sinners. Jesus said, "Lucifer, what have you got there?"

Satan replied, "I've got the world. I've got all mankind in this cage."

Jesus then asked, "What are you going to do with them?"

Satan replied: "I'm going to promise them everything. I'm going to promise them the moon. Then I'm going to break their hearts and damn their souls and send them into hell without God."

Jesus said, "Satan, I would like to have them."

"Jesus, You don't want them. They'll steal Your money. They'll desecrate Your day. They'll blaspheme Your name. They'll break Your promises. They'll dance in Your blood. They'll break Your heart. You don't want them."

Jesus replied, "I want them. I know the number of hairs on their heads. I know their names. I know their thoughts before they think them."

Satan said, "You will have to pay for them."

Jesus said, "I'll give you gold, the gold of all the universe."

Satan replied, "No, no, no. That is not enough."

"I'll give wealth untold—pearls, rubies, and all the mountains and all the oceans on the earth," came Jesus' reply.

"It is still not enough," said Satan.

"I'll give you diamonds and every continent on the earth and every island too. I'll give all of it to you in exchange for My people," Jesus said.

Satan replied, "That's not enough. That's not enough. I want more."

Then Jesus said, "All right, Lucifer. Name your price. What do you want?"

According to this legend, Satan smiled a wicked smile. "You wouldn't pay that price, Jesus," he said.

"Name your price, Lucifer," said Jesus.

"All right," said Lucifer, as his lips curled into a scowl. "I want the gold of Your heart. I want the diamonds of Your tears. I want the rubies of Your blood. I want You, Jesus. I want You on a cross. But You won't pay that price."

Then, without a word, Jesus began to lay aside His royal robes. He came to earth, lived a perfect life, and went to the old rugged cross and bled and died. He poured out His life on Calvary for every man, woman, boy, and girl, for whosoever would believe in Him.

For God so loved this world that He gave His own blood on the cross to open the door to heaven for you and me. He took the captive out of captivity. He turned bondage to freedom. He built a bridge back to heaven by the way of the Cross.

This message is still the same as it was yesterday. The Cross is the way by which all people can be saved and can still walk toward that glorious place called heaven.

Mercy's door is still ajar. The love of God is still available for all of us to experience. Each of us should pray this prayer: "Oh, God, thank You that Your love, which You showed in Jesus, shines on me too. Let that love come into my heart. I open my heart to You, Lord Jesus. Come in and be my Saviour too."

3
God Is
Unchangeable

For who is God save the Lord? Or who is a Rock save our God?
Psalm 18:31

In this age, it seems everything has come loose from its foundation. We hardly become acquainted with someone before he or she is telling us good-bye. We move constantly from neighborhood to neighborhood, from city to city, even from country to country. We find a political leader we like, and he passes so quickly from the scene that we can hardly believe that he was ever in the spotlight.

People change around us. They grow older. They change their hair colors. They change their vocations. They change their friends. Marriages are breaking up at an incredibly fast pace. Divorce seems epidemic. Children that seem happy suddenly run off and are swallowed up in the tide of prostitution and pornography that is sweeping our land.

Cities such as the one where I live—Houston, Texas—are changing at a rapid pace. People from northern cities are streaming out of those communities and are heading for the so-called Sunbelt. New suburbs spring up almost daily in fast-growing Sunbelt cities. Areas that once were the homes for the city's wealthiest residents decay and become dwelling places for the poor.

Economic conditions change all about us. I know business-men who have been on top of the world one day and at the bottom of bankruptcy the next morning. The stock market rises and falls, shaking off innocent speculators in its roller-coaster ride.

And look at all the changes that have come about just in this century: the airplane, the automobile, the spaceship, the computer, the microwave oven. These and thousands of other modern inventions have burst forth on our world in just a mere 80 years!

In this world of change, we often want to cry out, "Is there not something permanent? Is there not something we can rely on? Is there not something that is the same yesterday, today, and tomorrow?"

To this I answer yes, there is something, or rather Someone, who is unchanging. His name is God. He is the One who created us. He is the One who spoke the word that created this world. He is our Redeemer. He is the One who came to earth through the womb of a virgin to save us from ourselves and our sins. He is the One who is with His people every day, in the form of the Holy Spirit. This God does not change—not in the past, not now, not ever.

Even God's people in the world change. New churches are born. Old churches die. Pastors move on and are replaced by new ones. Church buildings deteriorate and must be remodeled, reconstructed, or replaced. Neighborhoods around churches change, and congregations are forced to relocate, expand, or shrink.

God's people grow old. They pass from one generation to the next.

But God does not change. Only God is the same as He was in the beginning and He will be the same at the end of time.

People Cry Out for God's Stability

Because of all these changes, we are an unsettled people. Our generation is fascinated with things that represent permanence and stability. Men and women today search frantically for pieces of antique furniture to buy and old houses and cars to acquire and restore. We search diligently through history and genealogical records looking for "roots" which signify our link with our far-distant past.

Our generation seeks something to give it meaning. An entire new field of literature has sprung up, of books which are nothing more than lists of facts. These facts have no commentary or explanation and are endless pages of data about mostly trivial and irrelevant things.

One phenomenon of our day is the wide interest in the *Guinness Book of World Records*. This is a meaningless list of trivia, which reports what certain people have done in excess. The biggest this and the tallest that are listed. The heaviest this and the oldest that are all catalogued in this book. The *Guinness* book gives us what we think we need: records, statistics, and facts which somehow seem to give our lives more importance.

Pop psychology is another fad of our day. There are as many different branches of psychology as there are psychologists in the field. Every one has his or her own pet theory about how to be one's own best friend or how to win through intimidation or how to make others pay attention.

Even in the field of religion there are fads galore. On every turn, some guru or spiritual master is offering some new technique—some new mantra—that is recommended to be repeated every so often in order to "free" one's spirit, whereas it really enslaves people to its far-out beliefs and demands.

In our society where everything is changing and where everyone seems to be reaching out for something permanent, we need to turn our eyes to the only part of our lives guaranteed not to change one iota. That Someone is God.

God's Laws Do Not Change

As the first American astronaut prepared to soar into space, one reporter asked, "What are you depending on most in your venture?" I suppose the reporter expected the astronaut to mention the great minds that created a reliable rocket and spaceship controls. Or maybe he thought the astronaut would boast about his own navigational skills. Instead, the astronaut replied, "That God will not change His laws." The astronaut knew that his life and the safety of his mission depended on God's laws. God created the laws of gravity, space, physics, and all of nature as well as the laws in the Old Testament.

This is precisely what the immutability—the permanence—of God is all about. God can be depended on to be what He has always been. His Word, His laws, His holiness, His sovereignty will not change. God—and the things of God—are the same yesterday, today, and forever. God does not invent new games and make new rules for each generation. A person can go to bed at night and get up in the morning, confident that he can pick up tomorrow where he left off the day before with God. People change their minds. People are often fickle. God does not change His mind. God is not fickle. God's love for us does not change. His laws for our world do not change. His conditions for accepting us do not change. His forgiveness does not change. The beautiful hymn says it well:

> Great is Thy faithfulness, O God my Father,
> There is no shadow of turning with Thee;
> Thou changest not, Thy compassions, they fail not;

As Thou hast been Thou forever wilt be.
Great is Thy faithfulness!
Great is Thy faithfulness!
Morning by morning new mercies I see;
All I have needed Thy hand hath provided.
Great is Thy faithfulness, Lord, unto me!
—Thomas O. Chisholm

The Key to God: the Bible

In the 1960s, rebellion flooded our streets. It spilled over into the early 1970s. The late 1970s became a time of deep introspection. It is unfortunate that many people turned to the new gurus and spiritual masters or to the latest pop psychology out of Hollywood. But many who sought these new philosophies soon found that they too were lacking in permanence and depth.

But the 1970s also saw a revival of interest in the Bible. The Bible is our only authentic record of God's actions in our world. Many people are hungry today to hear the old-time Word of God preached. They want to know what the Bible says and what the Bible means for today. They want to know that God still rules over this sin-sick, evil-infested world. They want to know that despite all the changes in our world and all of the world's upheavals and troubles, that God is still in control.

In my own church, which has grown to be the largest in Houston, Texas, I conduct a verse-by-verse exposition of the Bible every Sunday morning, Sunday night, and Wednesday night. Nearly 10,000 people a week come to hear these lessons. Nearly half of these left other churches that did not believe or teach the Bible. These churches of "What's Happening Now" have failed to connect people with God's Word and with God Himself. John MacArthur and Chuck Smith in California, W. A. Criswell in Dallas, and countless others across the country and around the world, are preaching to multiplied thousands each week who are tired of having their ears tickled with the latest philosophy and want to hear, "Thus saith the Lord."

The Bible is God's perfect record of Himself. In it, He tells us over and over that He can be counted on. The Bible is clear on these points: "He that keepeth thee will not slumber" (Ps. 121:3). Neither does He change. God's promises haven't changed. His love, His power, His forgiveness have not changed. And they never will.

The New Testament contains a story which describes in beautiful simplicity how the love of God never changes, despite people's efforts to run away and hide from Him. I refer to Jesus' parable about the Prodigal Son (Luke 15:11-32). In this story, the rebellious son departed with his share of his father's earthly possessions. He squandered all his wealth in a far country. Finally, the son came to his senses and returned to his father's house, confessed his sins and pleaded to be taken back. The father, of course, did just that—in the same way God lets us return to the fold after we wander. The rebellious son found a loving father waiting at the end of a long sinful journey, and we may find God waiting for us at the end of our sojourn in sin too. Even today, God and His people wait with open arms for rebellious sons and daughters, men and women, to return. The family of God—the church—still waits to welcome back sinners. As the father in the parable had not changed but still loved his son, God waits for you and me to return to Him.

I cannot promise you that your family will always feel toward you as they do today or as they did yesterday. I cannot promise that you will always be able to depend on your friends. But I can assure you that God never changes and He waits with open arms for His children, however steeped in sin they may be.

Other Religions Don't Teach This

When Jesus Christ was born, the prevailing world religion was Zoroastrianism. This religion taught that Ahriman, the god of darkness, and Ahura Mazda, the god of light, wrestled every day. A person who died on the day the god of light won went to a place like heaven. A person who died on a day in which the god of darkness prevailed went to hell. This is totally foreign to what the Bible teaches. God is *always* the Victor. Any person who dies trusting in Him will live with Him eternally.

Jesus taught that God's purpose is not born of caprice. Jesus did not teach that God throws matters into the air or settles issues by mere chance or whim. Our faith in God is not determined by some wrestling match that recurs daily. Our God has predetermined a wonderful plan for each of our lives. This plan, which culminates in the glorification of the believer, is based on the fixed, consistent, immutable nature of God. All things are ultimately determined by His intelligence, love, and sovereignty. God is the one stable factor in the universe and the Bible, the Word of God, is the accurate record of His immutable nature.

What God determines in His holiness and sovereignty, He accomplishes in His love and power. We can depend on God.

Jesus told another parable to illustrate the difference between placing our faith in an insecure, flimflam religion such as that of Zoroastrianism, versus a secure faith in the true God. This is the parable of the Wise and Foolish Builders. Said Jesus, "Whosoever cometh to Me and heareth My sayings, and doeth them, I will show you to whom he is like. He is like a man which built an house and digged deep, and laid the foundation on a rock; and when the flood arose, the stream beat vehemently upon that house and could not shake it; for it was founded upon a rock. But he that heareth, and doeth not, is like a man that without a foundation built an house upon the earth; against which the stream did beat vehemently, and

immediately it fell; and the ruin of that house was great"
(Luke 6:47-49).

When we place our faith in our God, who was the God of
Abraham, Isaac, and Jacob, and the Father of our Lord Jesus
Christ, we build our house upon the Rock. Amid this changing
world and the floods of life, our faith is secure. When our faith
is in God, it is as secure as the Rock of Gibraltar.

But when we place our faith in something as whimsical and
changing as a religion like Zoroastrianism or some modern
pop religion or some pop psychology or some current political
or religious leader, we are like the man who built his house
without a secure foundation. The changing world and life's
floods will sweep away the faith of a person whose faith is in
these things.

The Rock of our salvation is the eternal nature of God. He is
immutable, unchangeable. It is on this same foundation that
God's church is built.

In Psalm 18:2 we are told, "The Lord is my Rock and my
Fortress." And in Psalm 94:22 we read, "My God is the Rock of
my refuge." And in Psalm 89:26 God is described as "the Rock
of my salvation." These verses—and dozens of others like
them which liken God to a solid rock—show how secure our
faith is when it is founded on Him.

A foolish person builds his house upon the sands of time
and this world. A wise person builds his house on the solid
Rock which is our Lord and Saviour Jesus Christ.

Jesus also used this illustration of God as a secure Rock on
whom we can rely. We read of a discussion between Jesus and
His disciples: "When Jesus came into the coasts of Caesarea
Philippi, He asked His disciples, saying, 'Whom do men say
that I the Son of man am?'"

After they came up with three different but wrong ideas,
"Simon Peter answered and said, 'Thou art the Christ, the Son
of the living God.'

"And Jesus answered and said unto him, 'Blessed art thou, Simon Barjona, for flesh and blood hath not revealed it unto thee, but My Father which is in heaven. And I say also unto thee, that thou art Peter, and upon this rock I will build My church; and the gates of hell shall not prevail against it'" (Matt. 16:13-18).

The rock of our faith is the confession that Jesus is the Christ, the Son of the living God. On this confession—on this affirmation—we can rest assured of our eternal security, for it reflects our trust in God.

God told Moses that His name was "I Am." The Lord said, "I Am that I Am" (Ex. 3:14). In one of Jesus' strongest claims to deity, He taught that He was the same "I Am" who had spoken to Abraham (John 8:58).

When our trust is in Jesus Christ, it is also in our God, for the Father and the Son are One along with the Holy Spirit—one God in three forms all at the same time.

Darwin theorized that man evolved from animals. This is not so. Man is made in the image of the eternal God who does not improve with age, who does not mature in character or suffer mutations. God's immutability has its roots in His eternality. His changelessness is born of His eternal constancy. Because we are born of God and made in His image, we can know the inner stability of God. This is what it means to be "born again"—to become "new creatures," transformed and indwelt by no other than God Himself.

At conversion, the Holy Spirit becomes the "earnest" of our salvation. That means He becomes our "earnest money," or our "down payment," for our place in heaven. The Holy Spirit guarantees to us that God does not change. He pledges that if we trust in Him, through His Son, we will dwell with Him forever.

The stability, eternality, consistency, and changeless nature of God is necessary to our psychological and spiritual health.

And it can be experienced on a day-to-day basis in union with Him in whom we live and move and have our beings.

Though God's changelessness, strength, stability, grace, and power are imparted in spiritual and psychological health to millions, God remains whole. His grace toward us cannot drain Him of what He is. Jesus was no less man because He was God, and no less God because He was man. The changeless sufficiency of His being is not weakened because of our dependency on and union with Him. In sharing His holiness, sovereignty, power, love, mercy, and knowledge with finite man, God does not lessen Himself. His power remains unabated, His wisdom undiminished, His holiness untarnished, His strength inexhaustible.

God's Word is forever the same. His love is eternal. His mercy never ceases. God neither slumbers nor sleeps, yet He is never tired. All things are ours at the Father's hand, but the heavenly supply is never diminished. He meets all our needs according to His riches in glory by Christ Jesus, and His storehouse of blessings is never depleted.

While the Bible pictures God as unchanging, it depicts mankind as stars wandering out of their orbit. Mankind is presented as restless as the sea and as unstable as the waters (Isa. 57:20).

Our faith does not rest in mankind. Our faith must not be in ourselves. The wisest among us is ignorant compared with God. The richest among us is poor compared with God. The most beautiful among us is ugly compared with God. The smartest teacher will disillusion us. The finest preacher will fail us. The best spouse will disappoint us. Only God never changes. That is why we must preach and teach that God through Jesus Christ is the Rock of our salvation.

After the death of Elvis Presley, there was a rash of suicides among teenagers. When idols suffer, people suffer. When a member of a famous rock group gets a broken arm, some teenagers will break their arms deliberately.

In times of economic uncertainty, grown men and women will commit suicide because they have put their trust in stocks and bonds, in mortgages and collateral. And when these things of mankind become insecure, some who have put their faith in them become insecure and leap from buildings or lift revolvers to their heads.

In educational institutions some bright, intelligent students turn to suicide or mind-altering drugs when they are unable to make the grades that they and others expect of them.

Our trust must not be in rock stars, in money, in scholastic marks, or in other indications of achievement. Our trust must be in God.

We must believe in God, or else we will be disappointed. Only God is secure. Only God is unchanging.

4
God Is
Holy

Speak unto all the congregations of the Children of Israel, and say unto them, "Ye shall be holy; for I the Lord your God am holy."

Leviticus 19:2

God has one characteristic about which there can be no disagreement. The Bible clearly says that God is holy. "I am holy," says the Lord God (Lev. 11:44 and other verses).

This characteristic of holiness both describes God and sets Him apart from mankind. Few things or individuals in the Scriptures are called holy, and none of them are members of the human race. The Bible speaks of holy angels and holy days. In these cases, holy is used as an adjective and means that something is holy because it is a part of God, who is holy. Once God told Moses, "The place whereon thou standest is holy ground" (Ex. 3:5). Ground itself is not holy. But the ground where Moses stood was holy because God was present and Moses was in God's presence. God's people were commanded, "Remember the Sabbath Day, to keep it holy" (Ex. 20:8). Days are not holy in themselves. But the Sabbath was God's Day, and that is what made it holy. God's people were expected to honor that day, and in so doing, "to keep it holy."

In the Scriptures, the holiness of God is the backdrop against which the blight of human sin is mirrored. God's holiness helps us understand our own unholiness, and it should motivate us toward the mercy of God.

Any study of God's characteristics must logically begin with a look at the holiness of God. More than any other attribute, God's holiness is what sets Him apart from man. A discussion of holiness provides a microcosm of understanding about the vast differences between God and man, between the Creator and the created.

Holiness—Exclusive to God

What does it mean to say that God is holy? The answer is far-reaching and complex. It defies simple explanation.

First, let's discuss what holiness is *not*. It is not of human invention. Holiness is not of man. The high priest in the ancient Hebrew temple wore a band around his turban inscribed with the words, "Holiness unto the Lord." The priest was not trying to say that he was holy. He was saying that God is holy. Though the priest ministered before a holy God, he had no holiness of his own. Like all mankind, the priest had to make atonement for his own sin. Holiness is above sin. That which is sinful cannot be holy.

Only God and the things that are of God are sinless. As redeemed sinners, we are divine recipients of God's grace toward us. We are righteous only because we follow the holy God. The goodness we have is that granted by the grace of God. A believer stands justified before God, clothed in His righteousness, cleansed in His blood, covered by His imputed holiness. Redeemed sinners have no holiness of their own. Nothing about mankind itself may justly bear the title "holy."

So if holiness is not of man, where does it come from? The holiness of God is intrinsic within His nature. In other words, God's holiness is not something created, but it is a part of what makes Him God. If God were not holy, He would not be who He is.

God's holiness is not derived from another person, nor is it self-initiated or self-actuated. God did not acquire His holiness by man's decree or by heaven's ordination. He did not, at some point in His existence, decide to become holy. God, who is the great "I Am," possesses qualities of His nature which are eternal. Being holy is intrinsically, innately, inherently, and eternally a part of His nature.

Perhaps Webster's dictionary can help give us a handle on what it means to say that God is holy. Webster defines holy as "Characterized by perfection and transcendence; commanding absolute adoration and reverence." Pure holiness is beyond man. Holiness transcends man. Though it is beyond man, God's holiness demands man's attention in adoration and reverence.

Holiness—Goal of Redeemed People

The fact that people are not holy does not mean that we should not strive to become holy. In fact, the opposite is true. The inadequacy of man in his sin is not license to unholiness. Though a state of complete holiness and sinless perfection will not be realized in this life, it is the goal toward which the redeemed must continually and eternally press. God said, "Ye shall be holy, for I the Lord your God am holy" (Lev. 19:2). This should be the goal of every Christian's life. Even though we never attain perfect holiness in this life, it should still be the standard toward which all believers strive (1 Peter 1:15-16).

Some Christians teach that it is possible for redeemed people to reach a state of sinless perfection in this life. I do not agree. I believe that holiness should be the goal toward which we should strive. But in this life we will never fully attain perfection. Even if it were possible to reach a state of "sinless perfection" in this life, we still would not deserve the title "holy," for a truly holy person has never been imperfect or unholy. Holiness is eternal, inherent, and intrinsic within itself. The Bible says, "There is none holy as the Lord" (1 Sam. 2:2). No matter how hard we strive, we can never be as holy as God.

It will only be in heaven that we shall become holy. In heaven we will become something we have never been before—creations so complete that it may justly be said of us, "The former things are passed away." In heaven we will reach that completed state toward which we must continually strive here on earth. But we should not let this fact discourage us. Indeed, it should encourage us. In this life, we struggle with the world, the flesh, and the devil. Here we move from unholiness toward holiness. On earth, we strive toward holiness. But experientially we live in a world where our goal of holiness is "not yet." Nevertheless, we can trust that God, in His goodness and mercy, will someday complete this goal for us. In heaven, we shall live with God, surrounded by His holiness and transformed by it completely.

An Elusive Definition

Earlier we referred to Webster's definition of the word "holy." We said that definition would "help us get a handle on what it means to say that God is holy." We chose those words carefully because it is extremely difficult to give a precise definition of God's holiness. The word almost defies definition. The word that is translated "holy" and "holiness" in our English Bible comes from a Hebrew word that is impossible to define from its component parts. In most Greek or Hebrew words, we may take the sum of the parts comprising the finished word and learn its meaning. But the definition of "holy" cannot come from the Hebrew. The Hebrew definition can only describe the act or character of something or someone that is holy. To grasp the full meaning of holiness then, is to describe, not to define. It is interesting that our Lord so structured the word that it defies definition. I believe this was intentional. Like God Himself, God's holiness is more than we can ever describe or define fully in a book or in a sermon.

So back to our original question. What then does it mean to say that God is holy? We've already said that we cannot fully answer that question. We must learn to live with only a partial definition. We can only see how a holy God acts. We must remember, however, that God's holiness is much more than what we can ever hope to describe. We can say that our holy God is perfect and separate from that which is profane and evil. But this is only a beginning.

Understanding the elusiveness of the full definition of holiness will help show why Christians in this life cannot ever completely reach a state of holiness. A believer, moving from justification to glorification, presses toward the goal of holiness. Christians can and should reach out for the goal, striving for God's standard, though we cannot reach it in this life. Our spirits still inhabit unholy, fleshly bodies, contaminated by the presence of our old natures. Our old natures, though forgiven, are still operative and influence the new natures we receive at the time we invite Christ in our lives. We will become completely holy in heaven after we are rid of our old bodies and rid of the influences of our old natures. True holiness will come when, as totally new creatures, we will be living in our glorified state in heaven with God.

Grounds for Our Reverence of God

In this life, we may never be able to fully define God's holiness and we will never reach a state of complete holiness. But as the redeemed of God, we can learn to revere and to respect God's holiness, and to become more like Him.

God has created us so that after we sin, two things happen: first, we know that we have sinned. Within the soul of a believer is an intrinsic sense of guilt about sin. Christian men and women know when they have done wrong. They feel badly about what they have done after they have sinned. This is a natural fact of life. Conscience is a God-endowed capacity with which each person is born. We do not have to create it, though we may nourish it. We can, however, by neglect and rejection of its tug at our hearts, suppress and destroy it.

Not only do we feel guilty over the sin that is in our lives, but we also feel a need to make restitution for the wrong we have done. The second thing that happens after we sin is that we want to make it right. A sinful person is innately aware of the need to appease something outside of himself. And what do we want to appease? Quite naturally, we want to appease a being less sinful than ourselves. We have the desire—the need—to appease the One who is completely sinless. We have a need deep in our beings to want to be forgiven by God. Yes, we can reject this need inside of us. We can try to squelch it, to suppress it. But our need for forgiveness is still there.

This need to be forgiven is expressed in our worship of God. Thus, the most significant fact at the basis of all worship is that God is holy. His holiness demands that we seek His forgiveness. As unholy beings we do the most natural thing in life when we attempt to appease and become rightly related to the holy God. This need to appease—to reach out and touch—God is something that has characterized mankind down through the ages. Moses wanted to look in the face of God, but he was allowed only the opportunity of seeing God's back as He passed by. A psalmist pictured himself kneeling before the footstool of God, unable to approach the righteous God too closely (Ps. 99:5).

Man's Sin Magnifies God's Holiness

The incomprehensibility of the holiness of God is magnified by an adequate view of the unholy nature of sinful human beings. It is natural for man to prostrate himself before God, to grovel in the ground beneath the feet of the holy God. That very separation—God above and man below—becomes, in part, the ground or need to appease and worship Him. We should be eternally grateful to God for every manifestation of His holiness in Scripture, through conscience and through circumstance. Every time we face the fact of God's holiness and the gap between us and God, we grow more aware of our need for Him.

This point is at the heart of the Christian message. The Old Testament Law was not designed to separate us from God, but to point out how far we are from Him and how much we need Him. The Law was the schoolmaster to bring us to Christ (Gal. 3:24). Only the moral Law of God could reveal to us the mighty chasm between our sins and our sinless God.

We should thank God that "Where sin abounded, grace did much more abound" (Rom. 5:20). When God came in Christ and "the Word was made flesh" (John 1:14), God spanned the insurmountable gap between Himself and unholy man. It is indeed "amazing grace" that saved a wretch like me.

Holiness of God vs. Human Standards

Society will not survive indefinitely because people as a whole will not agree that God's holiness is the standard by which all people should live. All systems of moral, ethical, and governmental behavior should begin with the unalterable truth of God's holiness. If God's standard of perfection were accepted as the basic moral code of a government, there would be no room for situation ethics, optional lifestyles, and other forms of socio-philosophical nonsense that destroy a nation morally. The only standard on which a nation can keep on surviving is the standard of goodness, and God alone is good. So a system of government and law upon which longevity could be built would embody the innate moral goodness of God Himself.

The Ten Commandments are one window to the world of how God would act, if He were in our place. They are a picture of holiness against which our unholiness may accurately be mirrored. Legal experts tell us that the Ten Commandments have been incorporated into many of the world's greatest legal systems and provide a basis for law in our own civilization today. When Paul wrote, "All have sinned and come short of the glory of God" (Rom. 3:23), he recognized that God's holiness is the standard for all moral behavior, not just for Jews and Christians. God's own holy, glorious nature is the standard for measuring mortal beings who are created in His image.

Holiness Opposed to All Unholiness

God's holiness acts as a balance to other aspects of His nature, including His characteristic of love. Though He is a God of love, the Lord is constrained to set Himself completely against sin and sinners. Everything that God has created is set in motion against sin.

Though sinners sometimes think otherwise, mankind cannot live in opposition to God. A person cannot sin successfully. He opposes God and sets himself against the entire order of the universe. A person cannot do this and win. The odds have never been beaten. Neither you—nor I—can ever be the exception. If we break God's laws, we will suffer. God loves us and wants to redeem us. But God's holy nature will not tolerate our opposition to Him. If we love Him who first loved us, then we will want to become more like Him. We will want to strive to be like Him. As we've said before, people cannot become holy and perfect, but all Christians should strive toward that goal. That is what Paul urged us to do: "I beseech you therefore, brethren, by the mercies of God, that ye present your bodies a living sacrifice, holy, acceptable unto God, which is your reasonable service" (Rom. 12:1).

A person who chooses to work against God also chooses to work against the system of social order which God has "ordained" (Rom. 13:1) as an extension of His authority in the universe. From the cradle to the grave, a sinner fights against unbeatable odds. God cannot be defeated. No one can ever break the commandments of God and win. Like a ship battered around in a storm, a person who opposes God's laws is headed toward destruction.

"Why dost Thou show me iniquity, and cause me to behold grievance? For spoiling and violence are before me; and there are [those] that raise up strife and contention" (Hab. 1:3).

"And the men of Bethshemesh said, 'Who is able to stand before this holy Lord God? And to whom shall He go up from us?'" (1 Sam. 6:20)

To set yourself against God means you will be broken on the sea of life, smashed on the shore by a God who will not be mocked. The moral expression of God Himself through His universe is unalterable. He has no choice but to be against the sinner who chooses to be against Him.

Holiness Demands Clear-Cut Decisions
There should be no halfway, halfhearted reaction to the holiness of God. God does not want an unclear response to His holiness. The holiness of God demands clear-cut decisions.

Ours is a permissive society. The generation which precedes the second coming of Christ and the end of the world will be characterized by moral license and spiritual anarchy. Today we tend to excuse anything and explain away everything. But God, who made forever a great gulf between the rich man and Lazarus, has placed His unalterable standard of difference between the clean and the unclean. If you choose to live in habitual, premeditated, willful sin, you hang by a spider's thread over the mouth of hell, on a thread about to be burned in the middle by the candle of delay. It is a fearful thing to tempt the Lord. "Come out from among them and be ye separate, saith the Lord, and touch not the unclean thing" (2 Cor. 6:17).

The holiness of God ought to affect the way we live, for God demands a life that presses on toward perfection. The holiness of God should attract us toward God, not pull us away from Him. Sin is a willful act. It is an act of the will. We do not sin accidentally or unknowingly. We fool ourselves if we pray, "Forgive us of the sins we committed, and of those things we did that we did not know were sin." Sin is blatant rebellion against God and His holy nature and His holy style. God demands a difference in the lives of His people. Hear again the testimony of Isaiah: "In the year that King Uzziah died, I saw also the Lord sitting upon a throne, high and lifted up, and His train filled the temple. Above it stood the seraphims. Each one had six wings; with twain he covered his face, and with twain he covered his feet, and with twain he did fly. And one cried unto another, and said, 'Holy, holy, holy, is the Lord of hosts; the whole earth is full of His glory.' And the posts of the door moved at the voice of him that cried, and the house was filled with smoke. Then said I, 'Woe is me! For I am undone; because I am a man of unclean lips, and I dwell in the midst of a people of unclean lips; for mine eyes have seen the King, the Lord of hosts.' Then flew one of the seraphims unto me, having a live coal in his hand, which he had taken with the tongs from off the altar. And he laid it upon my mouth, and said, 'Lo, this hath touched thy lips; and thine iniquity is taken away, and thy sin purged.' Also I heard the voice of the Lord, saying, 'Whom shall I send, and who will go for Us?' Then said I, 'Here am I; send me'" (Isa. 6:1-8).

After Isaiah saw the holiness of God, he was never the same

again. Nothing, but nothing, will change our lives like an insight into God's holiness.

The Ground of Our Praise

The gap between God's holiness and our unholiness is great, but it can be bridged. By believing and trusting God, through Jesus Christ, the chasm between our unholiness and God's holiness can be crossed. Because of God's imputed righteousness, we can be justified before our holy God. God reaches out to us in love. For His amazing grace, let God be praised. God's grace and holiness are at the heart of our praise to Him. "He sent redemption unto His people; He hath commanded His covenant forever; holy and reverend is His name" (Ps. 111:9). God's Son shed His blood on the cross to save people from their sins and to move them from sinfulness toward holiness. Therefore, we should praise and have reverence for God forever.

When we think about praising our holy God, we must remember His amazing grace toward us, sinners that we are. What God is in holiness, we may become similar through His grace. One day we shall know as we are known, and live in perfect fellowship with Him. Let us give praise for the holiness of God and realize that His holiness is as important to our salvation as His amazing grace is to our worship. We cannot worship our holy God apart from the imputed righteousness of His amazing grace.

5

God Is
Merciful

For if ye turn again unto the Lord, your brethren and your children shall find compassion before them that lead them captive, so that they shall come again into this land. For the Lord your God is gracious and merciful, and will not turn away His face from you, if ye return unto Him.   *2 Chronicles 30:9*

Over and over in our Bible, the Lord our God is described as a God of mercy. In fact, there are almost as many references in the Bible to God's mercy as there are to His love.

Mercy and love are two separate characteristics, though sometimes they are confused or used interchangeably. The Bible says, "God commendeth His love toward us, in that, while we were yet sinners, Christ died for us" (Rom. 5:8). The Bible also says, "The Lord your God is gracious and merciful" (2 Chron. 30:9). Love describes a way God feels and acts toward us; mercy describes a way that God reacts to our condition.

Webster can be of some help in getting a grip on the differences between the words "love" and "mercy." The dictionary

defines love as "an affection based on admiration or benevo-
lence." It also says that love is "warm attraction." On the other
hand, mercy is described as "a compassion or forbearance
shown to an offender or subject." Moreover, it calls mercy "a
blessing that is an act of divine favor or compassion." Love,
then, is that feeling God has toward us, whom He has created.
Mercy, on the other hand, is an attitude God takes toward us
who are not worthy of His pardon.

The Lord our God is not only all-powerful, all-knowing,
ever-present, and loving, but He is also a God of mercy. Mercy,
then, is another strong characteristic of the God we love and
serve.

It is at the point of God's condescending mercy that He has
fellowship with us whom He has created. Our compassionate
and merciful heavenly Father is not only willing to forgive us,
but He is also slow to anger, plenteous in mercy, and the
Initiator of all grace. By every rule of the book, it would seem
that a sinful offender would need to devise ways by which to
approach God and to plead for mercy. Yet precisely the opposite is true. The Bible portrays a loving heavenly Father who is
seeking us, pleading with us to receive His offer of divine
mercy and forgiveness.

As the Prophet Jeremiah put it, "It is of the Lord's mercies
that we are not consumed, because His compassions fail not.
They are new every morning; great is Thy faithfulness"
(Lam. 3:22-23).

The Psalmist David wrote:

The Lord is merciful and gracious, slow to anger, and plenteous
in mercy. He will not always chide; neither will He keep His
anger forever. He hath not dealt with us after our sins, nor
rewarded us according to our iniquities. For as the heaven is
high above the earth, so great is His mercy toward them that
fear Him. As far as the east is from the west, so far hath He

removed our transgressions from us. Like a father pitieth his children, so the Lord pitieth them that fear Him. For He knoweth our frame; He remembereth that we are dust. As for man, his days are as grass; as a flower of the field, so he flourisheth. For the wind passeth over it, and it is gone; and the place thereof shall know it no more. But the mercy of the Lord is from everlasting to everlasting upon them that fear Him, and His righteousness unto children's children (Ps. 103:8-17).

Mercy Means "to Relieve the Miseries"

In the Bible the expressions goodness, loving-kindness, and mercy are sometimes used interchangeably. One of the most consistently used word-pictures for mercy is that of a fine, noble person stepping from his lofty position to help someone who is inferior. "To relieve the miseries" may be the best way to state that characteristic of God which causes Him to extend mercy on our behalf.

Sometimes we say we show mercy to an injured animal by putting him out of his misery. I am grateful that our Lord doesn't usually relieve our miseries in that way! We humans express our "mercy" to hurt animals in this way when there is nothing else we can do for them. That, of course, is not the way it is with God. He has the power to change our situations. God can show mercy to us in ways that we humans only wish we could express.

In the Old Testament, the point at which God expressed His love in the forgiveness of sin was at a place called "the mercy seat." Here the high priest annually placed the blood of a sacrificial lamb so that the holy God might show mercy to His sinning people. It is at the point of condescending mercy that God has fellowship with people.

The term "mercy seat" of God was also a dramatic, visual way of pointing out God's characteristic of mercy. God was present in the ancient temple because of His mercy, which He was willing to show toward Israel. The Bible even gives a description of what this seat looked like:

> Thou shalt make a mercy seat of pure gold: two cubits and a half shall be the length thereof, and a cubit and a half the breadth thereof. And thou shalt make two cherubims of gold, of beaten work shalt thou make them, in the two ends of the mercy seat. And make one cherub on the one end, and the other cherub on the other end; even of the mercy seat shall ye make the cherubims on the two ends thereof. And the cherubims shall stretch forth their wings on high, covering the mercy seat with their wings, and their faces shall look one to another; toward the mercy seat shall the faces of the cherubims be. And thou shalt put the mercy seat above upon the ark; and in the ark thou shalt put the testimony that I shall give thee. And there I will meet with thee, and I will commune with thee from above the mercy seat, from between the two cherubims which are upon the ark of the testimony, of all things which I will give thee in commandment unto the Children of Israel (Ex. 25:17-22).

The hymn of comfort, "Come Ye Disconsolate," speaks of this mercy seat as a place of solace:

> Come, ye disconsolate, where-e'er ye languish,
>   Come to the mercy seat, fervently kneel;
> Here bring your wounded hearts, here tell your anguish;
>   Earth has no sorrow that heaven cannot heal.
> —Thomas Moore

Mercy is also much more than just an action. To show mercy is to act in ways that are not required. God does not have to accept sinful people. God's perfection could cause Him to shun His imperfect creatures. But because of His mercy God literally reaches down and touches us who do not deserve such treatment from the Holy Being.

Love, Mercy, and Grace

Grace is the means by which the holy God expresses His love and mercy to an unholy creation. God focuses on what we do not deserve and cannot do for ourselves. Justice is what we deserve, but mercy is what He chooses to bestow on us.

The holiness of God demands satisfaction and judgment. Because God is perfect and holy, we sinners are not worthy of being in His presence, let alone living with Him forever. God's holiness demands that we die, because we have failed. We are not what we should be. We are not perfect as our Father in heaven is perfect.

The only satisfaction to both God's love and His holiness is the Cross, where God Himself expressed His love for us in the gift of His Son, while satisfying the divine justice of His holiness by condemning sin in the flesh. In other words, God's holiness demanded a perfect sacrifice because of mankind's unholiness. But God's love demanded that He spare His imperfect creations. God's holiness and sovereignty must be understood in the context of His loving and gracious personality. The Cross extends up to heaven and down to humanity, reconciling trusting people with their God. And divine justice is satisfied. The Bible says, "The wages of sin is death, but the gift of God is eternal life" (Rom. 6:23). Because God is holy and perfect, and we are not, we deserve to die. But because God loved the world so much, "He gave His only begotten Son, that whosoever believeth in Him should not perish, but have everlasting life" (John 3:16). Because God loved the world, He meted out mercy.

Gospel songwriter William R. Newell has written of God's mercy so eloquently:

> Years I spent in vanity and pride,
> Caring not my Lord was crucified.
> Knowing not it was for me He died
> On Calvary.

> Mercy there was great, and grace was free;
> Pardon there was multiplied to me.
> There my burdened soul found liberty,
> At Calvary.

This is a song about mercy—God's mercy. We sinners do not deserve anything better than death. But through Jesus Christ, God has given us much, much more. He has given us life eternal.

The Cross stands as the all-time monument to God's holiness, sovereignty, justice, judgment, power, immutability, love, mercy, and grace. The Cross is another way of saying "God's mercy." At the Cross, God literally reached down and "paid the price" for my sins and your sins.

Mercy Is Unique to Our God

People are incurably religious. Everything that people know to be stronger than their selfhood, they personify and deify. So people have created gods of sex and appetite, gods of persuasion and envy, and gods of war and peace.

Standing within the Agora, between the Acropolis and Mars Hill, the Apostle Paul was aghast at the abundance of pagan gods he saw. There were gods of Cercrops, Minerva, Vista, Diana, Hercules, Thesmus, Thadmus, and Zeus, not to mention the Deorama, the very personification of the Roman Empire itself, plus many others.

Even today there are many gods in our world. Some are shiny new four-wheel vehicles. Some are beautiful movie starlets whose torrid love-lives capture our attention and interests. Some are the dollars we carry in our pockets or stash away in bank vaults or in investments.

Some of the gods mankind has created have pictured the ugly horror of vindictive, angry, heathen deities, the personification of human fears, and the embodiment of human wrath. Yet the Athenians had an altar "to the unknown god." And it was of this god that Paul spoke, when he said, "Whom . . . ye ignorantly worship, Him I declare unto you" (Acts 17:23).

In the midst of people's search for gods to worship, there is the one true, living God whom we should worship. Paul told the Athenians that their unknown God was indeed this God, for He was what they were searching for. Even today, our God is the One whom many are unknowingly searching for.

Our need to be religious, then, points us in the direction of the one true, living God. But we must be wary lest we fall victim to the many false, unreal gods the world constantly offers.

Only our God is truly merciful. All the other gods offer nothing but false hope and empty promises. The Gospel writers affirm with one accord that God alone is true mercy incarnate. Full of grace and compassion, slow to anger, willing to forgive, plenteous in mercy. These are all characteristics of the Lord our God.

Jesus stepped into a world that understood God only in terms of a caustic, angry Being, who took great delight in holding sinners over the flaming pits of hell. But though God does punish, He is a loving Father. He is not unrelenting. He will not always chide, or hold us in hot displeasure. But God does not forgive the unforgiving, those who do not forgive others for their shortcomings (Matt. 18:35). People who are not merciful to others forfeit God's mercy (Matt. 5:7). Jesus illustrated this facet of God's personality when He told the Parable of the Talents (Matt. 18:23-25). In this story, a man owed a king a large debt. The man could not pay, so the king ordered that he and his family be sold. The man pleaded for mercy, and the king forgave him his debt and ordered him released. The forgiven man then went out and tried to collect a much smaller debt from someone who owed him money. When the second debtor could not pay, he too asked for mercy. But the man who had been forgiven of his huge debt by the king had the second man seized and thrown into debtors' prison. When the king found out what had happened, he had the first man thrown into debtor's prison too. The point of this story is clear: forgiveness begets forgiveness. The pardoned must learn to pardon others, or they jeopardize their own pardon. Obviously this parable is a clear reference to God as the King. God has forgiven us of so much; therefore, we in return must forgive others. We do not forgive *in order* to be forgiven; we forgive *because* we are forgiven.

Jesus also illustrated God's merciful spirit when He encountered a woman taken in adultery. He did not condemn her. He said, "Neither do I condemn thee. Go, and sin no more" (John 8:11).

God, who at sundry times and in diverse means, revealed Himself through the heavens, peoples' consciences, the Law, and the Prophets, later revealed Himself in Jesus Christ (Heb. 1:1-2). That revelation is love personified. It is mercy incarnate. Unique to our God alone is the characteristic of a merciful personality.

Transferable Mercy

Grace is the exclusive avenue through which God forgives sin and extends His hand of mercy to mankind. It follows, therefore, that mercy is the most naturally transferable attribute of God to His own. Because God is merciful, we may also be merciful. Actually His words are stronger than that: because God is merciful, we *must* also be merciful. A person who will not show mercy will not know mercy. He who is not able to forgive will not be forgiven. The mercy of God, then, is not to be understood in mere theological terms, but in experience. Mercy is a series of actions, not merely a quality of character.

We live in a world filled with people who desperately need mercy from those who have experienced mercy. The world is hardly interested in our theological positions, but is responsive to our compassion as children of God. I believe it can be proven that governments whose peoples have been touched with the Christian Gospel are more merciful than governments which oppose the Gospel. Why has America sought for over 200 years to champion underdogs? It is surely because of the influence of the Gospel and the fact that the teachings of Jesus Christ are deeply imprinted upon many in our country. Showing mercy is a cornerstone of the Gospel. Therefore, we still show mercy as a nation because we know the mercy of our Father in heaven.

Mercy as a Fruit of the Spirit

Mercy is not just an attribute of God; it is also a prominent Christian attribute. God's people should be known for their merciful attitudes.

The Apostle Paul has written of two manifestations of the indwelling Spirit of Christ in the lives of believers. One is the gifts of the Spirit (1 Cor. 12, e.g.). The other is the fruit of the Spirit (Gal. 5:22-23). When Paul referred to the Spirit, he meant the work and ministry of Christ. When he referred to the fruit of the Spirit, he meant the personality and character of Christ as evidenced in a Christian's life. In Romans 12:8 mercy is listed as a gift of the Spirit. In Galatians 5:22, goodness, which may also be translated "mercy," is listed as a fruit of the Spirit. Because God is merciful, Jesus Christ ministered in mercy. Mercy is the only gift of the Spirit specifically declared to have expressed itself in the personality of Christ, and it may indeed be the greatest expression of His being.

So what does it mean for a Christian to express mercy in his lifestyle? Let us not confuse a merciful attitude with softness. Much as some people misunderstand God's love as meaning that He has no other characteristics, so we must not misunderstand God's mercy as meaning that He is just a pushover. Because God loves does not mean He is a softy. Though God forgives confessed sin, He does not wink at sin. He stares it straight in the face and denounces it, but He forgives believers who ask Him for His forgiveness.

The grace of God is free but it isn't cheap. It cost God everything to express His love toward us in terms of mercy. It cost Him His only begotten Son, our Lord and Saviour Jesus Christ. For without the Cross to satisfy the sovereignty of God and the terms of His justice, God could never have extended His mercy toward us through His grace.

Because of the death of Jesus Christ on the cross of Calvary, believing sinners are forgiven and set free from the bondage of sin. At conversion a guilty sinner goes free, but his guilt of sin is dealt with. A penitent believer does not pay for his guilt; Someone else has paid for it. The Bible makes it clear that the wages of sin is death. And the Bible makes it equally clear that all of us have sinned and fallen short of God's standards. The Someone who paid the price for each of us is Jesus Christ. Jesus paid our purchase price. As Gospel songwriter Elvina Hall put it:

> Jesus paid it all,
> All to Him I owe.
> Sin had left a crimson stain,
> He washed it white as snow.

So you see, because of God's mercy Jesus paid our price. It was because of God's mercy that Jesus died.

God is *against* everything that sin is *for*. All paganism, the occult, sins, rebellion, and immorality are themselves against Christ and the Cross. In the blackest hour of history Jesus Christ, "who knew no sin," became sin for us (2 Cor. 5:21).

The mercy of God is revealed to mankind at the cost of the greatest sacrifice the world has ever known. "For God so loved the world, that He gave His only begotten Son, that whosoever believeth in Him should not perish, but have everlasting life" (John 3:16).

God's judgment is an act of mercy. God loves us and wants the best for us. The greatest gift which He gave to people was the capacity to choose Him. This sets us above the animals. The most important feature of the creature made in the image of the Creator is his capability of choice. When a person chooses to go away from God rather than toward God, even the facts of death and hell reflect God's love and mercy. For God will not force anyone to love Him.

We are free to choose God or to reject Him. God does not stand over us and make us choose Him. This freedom is a great gift. But it has its price. If we choose right, we gain eternity. If we choose wrong, we lose eternity.

Some sinners wait uselessly to see if God will "do something" to them if they sin. I've heard people who have denied God stand up and say, "I have rejected God, but look how I prosper. In the eyes of Christians, I appear to be a dreadful sinner, but look at how well I am doing."

I want to tell people who say that, "Just wait. God still rules heaven and earth. He will have the final say." Sin has its own built-in punishment. A compassionate God expressed His love for mankind by simply allowing a person who has chosen to go away from Him to continue going on farther and farther away from Him, right through this life and into the next. Remember the old expression, "Give a person enough rope and he'll hang himself"? I like to rephrase that saying a little: "Give a sinner enough time, and he'll end up destroyed by his own game." Eternal perdition, then, itself becomes a monument to the loving God who will never force Himself upon His created beings.

This freedom baffles some folk. They somehow or another want God to always throw out a lifeline and love all sinners so much that He will never let anyone suffer the natural consequences of his actions. But the opposite is true. God loves us so much that He is willing to give us the freedom to choose for ourselves. And in giving us the freedom, He is true to us and to Himself and His Word. What God says He will do, He will do. If He says He gives us the freedom to choose, then He gives us that freedom. We would not have real freedom if God made the choices for us.

It must be clearly understood that while God loves us too much to force us to turn from our sinful ways and to enjoy Him forever in heaven, there is a point beyond which we may not go in our capacity to exercise choice. When one does not choose God's way, one turns away from eternal salvation and life with God forever. There will come a day in such people's lives when it will be too late to go back and make the choice differently. "Now is the accepted time; behold, now is the day of salvation" (2 Cor. 6:2).

If the reader of this page knows in his heart that he is, as yet, unpenitent and unconverted, let him turn to the Lord now. God's mercy is reaching down to all of us, through His grace. He wants all of us to make the choice to live and love Him forever. But He has given us the option; the choice is ours to make. We either claim or reject His mercy.

6
God Is
Just

Tell ye, and bring them near; yea, let them take counsel to-gether. Who hath declared this from ancient time? . . . Have not I the Lord? And there is no God else beside Me; a just God and a Saviour; there is none beside Me.   *Isaiah 45:21*

For the righteous Lord loveth righteousness; His countenance doth behold the upright.   *Psalm 11:7*

For therein is the righteousness of God revealed from faith to faith. As it is written, "The just shall live by faith."
Romans 1:17

The courts in our land are dedicated to establishing justice for our people. One symbol we use for justice is a blindfolded woman holding up the balance scales of justice. God does not have to be blindfolded to offer justice. His just and righteous nature work constantly to balance the scales of justice for His creation.

When we speak of God as just, it is another way of saying that God is righteous. The same Hebrew word forms the basis for both the English words "justice" and "righteousness."

So what does it mean to say that our Lord is a just or righteous God? It means that God's ways are the very essence of justice. God is the groundspring out of which all justice and righteousness flow.

God is the definition of what it means to do justly and walk uprightly. When we speak of God as just, it is also another way of saying that God is fair. In His love, He is compassionate. In His holiness, He is set apart from mankind. In His sovereignty, He is absolute Ruler. But as just or righteous, God is also our example of justice and fairness.

According to N. H. Snaith in *A Theological Word Book of the Bible*, "'Righteousness' involves the establishment of equal rights for all, and to this extent 'justice' is a same equivalent. The word is actually used in a sense of giving judgment, and God does judge righteously."

As a just God, our God is generous as well as benevolent. He exhibits loving-kindness as well as understanding. He does not demand what we are incapable of giving, but instead He gives us what we are incapable of getting or finding on our own.

God Is Our Judge

When we say that God is just, we recognize that God is our Judge. Many people believe they can live their own lives and commit all sorts of sins and never get caught. They may not get caught in this life, but their sins will catch up with them someday. God keeps a record of all that we do. He knows if we cheat on our income taxes. He knows if we are unfaithful to our spouses. He knows if we lie to our neighbors. He knows if we steal things. In His omniscience, God knows all things.

We may think that we can deceive God, but we cannot. We may not be found out in this life, but we will be exposed on the day that we stand before God, our Creator, Redeemer, and Judge.

Do you believe in a final judgment for all persons? Jude wrote, "Behold, the Lord cometh with 10 thousands of His saints, to execute judgment upon all, and to convince all that are ungodly among them of all their ungodly deeds which they have ungodly committed, and of all their hard speeches which ungodly sinners have spoken against Him" (vv. 14-15).

If you don't believe in a final judgment, you do not believe the Bible. Repeatedly throughout the Bible are references to the fact that each one of us will someday stand before the just God and make an accounting for our sins in this world. For example, the Bible asks, "Who shall give account to Him that is ready to judge the quick and the dead?" (1 Peter 4:5) Someday God will judge not only the living but the dead, who shall be raised by Christ for the final judgment.

Because God is just, He will make a judgment on each one of us. That judgment will be just, for God will note whether our sins have been forgiven. His judgment will be swift. It will be final. God will say to those who don't know Him, "Depart from Me" (Matt. 25:41). But those who trust in Him will be invited to live with Him forever (Matt. 25:34).

On what will God's judgment of us be made? On our deeds in this world? No! On how much money we have made? No! Or on the basis of how much money we have given away? No! Or on how many Sunday School classes we have taught? No! Or on the basis of how many churches we have started? No!

To all these, our answer is, "No!" Our judgment will be based on our faith in Jesus Christ, the only begotten Son of the Father, who for us sinners became man and died and was resurrected, so that we might have life eternal (1 John 5:11-13).

Over and over in the Old and New Testaments we are told of God's righteousness and His just ways. Because God is just, He is at work, constantly justifying more sinners to Himself.

The greatest indication of the just nature of our God was the birth, life, death, and resurrection of His Son, our Lord and Saviour Jesus Christ. God has taken His just nature and justified us to Himself through Jesus. As Paul wrote, "Therefore being justified by faith, we have peace with God through our Lord Jesus Christ" (Rom. 5:1).

We can best understand the just nature of God by focusing our attention on His action of justification through Jesus Christ. Because God is just, He can bring us into a state of justification.

The Wages of Sin Is Death

Christians know that the wages of sin is death, but the gift of God is eternal life (Rom. 6:23). This expression beautifully describes the justice of God. The wages of sin is death and separation from God. But God gave His Son, Jesus Christ, to be the substitute Payment for our sins. Faith in God's Substitute brings about the mighty transformation called conversion. When we stand before God in judgment, we stand condemned, unless we have faith in Jesus Christ. If we have faith in Jesus Christ, we will stand before God in judgment as redeemed people. The key factor in God's judgment, then, is faith in Jesus Christ. If we have faith in Christ, God's just nature allows us to stand in a state of justification before Him (Acts 13:39).

But if we stand before God without Christ, we have no hope. Though God is a just God, there is no way we can ever hope to earn His favor or salvation. If the total activities of our lives were placed on God's scales of righteousness, we would all be found deficient. We cannot do enough good things in this life to compensate for our sins. Not one of us is near enough to perfection to escape the wrath of God.

Do you remember what Jesus told the Pharisees? Many of these men in Jesus' day thought they were righteous because they followed the exact details of the Law of Moses. But Jesus reminded them that even in their self-righteousness they too were not perfect—in fact, far from it. The Pharisees felt they were righteous because they had not, for example, committed murder or adultery. But Jesus reminded them that the thoughts of their hearts were as sinful in the eyes of God as those actions of the flesh. Jesus reminded all of us that when we hate someone, we commit spiritual murder. He reminded all of us that when we lust, we commit adultery in our hearts.

By God's standards, not one of us—no, not one—can claim to be innocent. We may not commit certain sins, but we each have our own sins that we have committed. They may not be sins that others can readily point to, but God knows what they are. Pride, hate, jealousy, and deception are only a few of the sins that destroy us inwardly. God knows the thoughts in our minds, the intentions in our hearts. We may fool each other, but we cannot fool God. God's standard of measure is much higher than we can reach.

A just God wants to find all of us innocent. He wants to give us all fair trials. But because He is just, God cannot simply overlook the bad facts about our lives. He takes each fact and weighs it carefully. He knows the circumstances and the reasons behind our actions. But the just God knows that we are not capable by ourselves of tilting the scales of justice in our favor.

Justification Is by Faith in Christ

Let us focus now on what it means to be justified through faith in Jesus Christ. The word justify means to stand in a state of righteousness before God. It is just as though I had never sinned. Justification is a state, a standing, a possession of righteousness wherein I appear in the Father's eyes in a state of absolute perfection on the basis of His imputed righteousness. If we are justified, we are "accepted in the beloved" (Eph. 1:6).

Someone has said:

> Repentance is a change of mind about God.
> Conversion is a change of nature from God.
> Justification is a change of standing before God.
> Adoption is a change into the family of God.
> Sanctification is a change of service for God.
> Glorification is a change into likeness with God.

There are four key areas we should remember about our justification:

1. *Justification is a change in my standing before His eyes.* Before Christ, before conversion, I had no standing at all. Everything about me was anti-God and anti-Christ. I was against the entire created order of the universe. As a rebel against the authority of heaven, I shook my moral fists in the face of the Almighty and cried with Satan, "Down with God. I will be my own God. I will join with the sons of men and we shall do our own thing."

In his second Thessalonian letter, the Apostle Paul referred to the "mystery of iniquity," that illogical force of evil which permeates human hearts at every extremity of society. As a sinner I was acquainted with the "mystery of iniquity" (2 Thes. 2:7), stated independence from God, and made my "declaration of war" on the God of all creation. And God laughed (Ps. 2:4). He that shall smite the nations with a rod of iron, marveled that such an insignificant creature as I would despise Him, defy Him. And I stood alone before my God. Naked, bankrupt, defenseless, hopeless, puny, pitiful, lost. Undone and alone was I. And without Christ to help. My days were numbered. My destiny sealed. My destruction interminably, irrevocably fixed. My standing before God? I had no standing at all.

Without friend or Father, without advocate or defense, I

stood embarrassed and helpless before the all-seeing eye of His justice. But then, oh glorious day, He sought me, wooed me, and won my heart. And now I am a new creature. *"Old things are passed away."* Now everything is different (2 Cor. 5:17), and best of all, I stand before Him complete, clothed in His righteousness, just as if I had never sinned.

Volumes could be written on the theological aspects of justification, but it is, simply stated, that I stand complete in Him, clothed in His righteousness, accepted in the Beloved as though I had never been what I was before.

To say that in the mind of God I stand positionally in a state as though I had never sinned at all is beyond all human comprehension. Is not God all-knowing? Does He who knows all things that shall be, remember all things that have been? It is at this point that we must remind ourselves of the omniscience and omnipotence of God.

Yes, on the one hand He knows all things, while on the other He can do all things. If He is sovereign and does what He wants, and if He is omnipotent and has the power to do as He wills, then does it not stand to reason that He is able to forget that which He chooses? And what does He choose to forget? The confessed and forgiven sins of the penitent!

God casts our sins behind His back and they become as distant as the east is from the west (Ps. 103:12), and He remembers them against us no more. In His Trinitarian expression our God can be in one place and yet be everywhere at once. That is, indeed, a truth beyond finite comprehension. Just so, our God can remember everything and yet forget that which He chooses. And He chooses to forget the sins I have remembered to confess to Him. It is a thought both marvelous and mysterious, but nonetheless wonderfully true. God does not remember sins confessed by His children.

So vividly has this truth been etched on my soul, so deeply do I believe it, that I believe with all my heart that were I to ask Him, "Father, do You remember the sin I confessed to You yesterday?" that my God, were He to reply audibly, would respond, "No, I don't remember it at all. What sin are you talking about?"

Justification, glorious doctrine that it is, may well be the most important of the great doctrines of salvation relative to my position in Christ now and through eternity.

2. Justification is authenticated by His life. The Book of Romans is the believer's handbook on the doctrine of salvation. Its theme of justification by faith states simply that a believer stands before God exclusively on the basis of an imputed righteousness, having no real righteousness of his own. "Therefore, [Abraham's belief in God] was counted unto him for righteousness" (Rom. 4:3).

As Abraham believed what God had said, we too are urged to stand alone by faith in what God has done for us in His Son. Salvation is "for us also, to whom it shall be imputed if we believe" (Rom. 4:24). The basis of our standing before God is an imputed righteousness predicated on our faith in the death and resurrection of Jesus Christ.

But it is not simply that one died; rather *who* it is that died is what counts. Jesus "was delivered for our offenses and was raised again for our justification" (Rom. 4:25). And who is He that was delivered? He is the Son of God by whose death we are reconciled and by whose life we shall be saved (Rom. 5:10). What does the apostle mean by the expression, "We shall be saved by His life"? The perfection of Jesus' life made possible the vicarious nature of His death and death-defying resurrection. Had Jesus not lived a perfect life, He could not have died a perfect death for imperfect people. If His life would not have been sinless there would not have been any resurrection from the dead and no continuing life to perpetuate our standing in grace. Were He not perfect, the Cross would have meant nothing. He had to be perfect to die for my imperfection, and only the Son of God could be perfect. And as the Son of God, He alone could rise for our justification.

3. My justification is validated by His resurrection. Jesus lived a perfect life as the Son of God, giving efficacy to His atonement on the cross and power to His resurrection. But there is more, much more than that, in the continuing nature of His saving life. He "was delivered [over to death] for our offenses and raised again for our justification" (Rom. 4:25). In this expression Paul referred to the saving work of Christ in the nature of His high priestly office. The Jewish high priest on the Day of Atonement killed the Passover lamb to make possible the pardon of the guilt of the people from their sins.

But mark my words: *"to make possible."* The lamb slain, and its shed blood, provided no cleansing from sin. It only made possible that cleansing. Were the high priest to stop short of fulfilling all of his obligations, the potential provision in the sacrifice would never be effective. With the sacrifice of the lamb, his work was only half completed. Eagerly the people waited as the high priest disappeared behind the veil of the tabernacle in the holy of holies where he applied the blood on the mercy seat of the altar.

Atop the mercy seat two cherub statues faced each other. At the point at which their eyes met, God met man. And there the blood had to be placed. Forever God would have us know that the only point at which the holy God meets unholy people is at the point of innocent blood. Those people who had faith in the work of the high priest in their behalf received instant imputation for their sins.

On the cross our Lord, as God's Passover Lamb, made the once-for-all perfect sacrifice for the sins of the world. He was crucified for our sins—He was delivered for our offenses. But that was not enough. He who would be our once-for-all Sacrifice must become our once-for-all Priest. Listen again to Paul's statement: He "was delivered for our offenses, and was raised again for our justification" (Rom. 4:25).

For when Moses had spoken every precept to all the people according to the Law, he took the blood of calves and of goats, with water, and scarlet wool, and hyssop, and sprinkled both the book, and all the people, saying, "This is the blood of the testament which God hath enjoined unto you." Moreover he sprinkled with blood both the tabernacle, and all the vessels of the ministry. And almost all things are by the Law purged with blood; and without shedding of blood is no remission. It was therefore necessary that the patterns of things in the heavens should be purified with these; but the heavenly things themselves with better sacrifices than these. For Christ is not entered into the holy places made with hands, which are the figures of the true; but into heaven itself, now to appear in the presence of God for us. Nor yet that He should offer Himself often, as the high priest entereth into the holy place every year with blood of others; for then must He often have suffered since the foundation of the world; but now once in the end of the world hath He appeared to put away sin by the sacrifice of Himself (Heb. 9:19-26).

And every priest standeth daily ministering and offering oftentimes the same sacrifices, which can never take away sins. But this Man, after He had offered one sacrifice for sins forever, sat down on the right hand of God; from henceforth expecting till His enemies be made His footstool. For by one offering He hath perfected forever them that are sanctified (Heb. 10:11-14).

Herein is the glorious truth of the completed work of Christ for our justification. Not only did He die as the Passover Lamb, but He rose as our High Priest to ascend into the heavenlies and enter the holy of holies not made with hands, to sprinkle His own blood on the mercy seat in heaven, and this—once for all.

In the holy of holies was no chair, for the priest was never seated, indicating that his work was never done. But Jesus, after He sprinkled the mercy seat in heaven, forever sat down at the right hand of God. Let 10,000 hallelujahs ring! Our High Priest, crucified for our sins, has been raised for our justification. If we believe, we are saved because His perfect life authenticated His work on the cross. And we are saved by the continuing life He now lives at the right hand of the Father where He ever lives to make intercession for us.

4. *Justification is imputed by faith.* Justification is imputed to believers. It is imparted from God to those who will have it on the basis of faith. It is given to all who "believe on Him that raised up Jesus our Lord from the dead" (Rom. 4:24).

A troubled Martin Luther found rest for his longing soul when he nailed his faith to the peg of Romans 5:1-2: "Therefore being justified by faith, we have peace with God, through our Lord Jesus Christ; by whom also we have access by faith into this grace wherein we stand, and rejoice in hope of the glory of God."

It is by faith we are saved, and in faith we stand justified before God (Eph. 2:8-9). You are not saved by your good life, if you have one, nor are you kept by it. You are no more converted by your own effort than you stand justified by it. We are the humble recipients of God's grace. He has done for us what we could never do for ourselves. You can be baptized, you can live a good life, you can do your service, but it is to no avail if you do it in order to justify yourself to the holy God. God's Son was crucified for our sins; He was raised for our justification.

Justification is God's work. The Bible says, "We are His workmanship, created in Christ Jesus unto good works" (Eph. 2:10). We are not saved *by* good works; we are saved *unto* good works. Let our justified life bear fruit to the glory of Him who has pronounced us "accepted in the beloved" (Eph. 1:6).

Because our God is just, because our God is righteous, we can be redeemed. Our just God has provided an avenue—

justification by faith in Jesus Christ—for us all. It is so easy; we only need to believe. God takes care of the rest!

God Is
All-Knowing

For the Word of God is quick, and powerful, and sharper than any two-edged sword, piercing even to the dividing asunder of soul and spirit, and of the joints and marrow, and is a discerner of the thoughts and intents of the heart. Neither is there any creature that is not manifest in His sight; but all things are naked and opened unto the eyes of Him with whom we have to do. Hebrews 4:12-13

Many companies today are building marvelous new computers. These machines have the capacity to store startling amounts of information. These computers can sort through millions of pieces of information and reorganize the individual tidbits of facts in a variety of ways and in only a few minutes. For instance, one computer can store the names and addresses of every automobile owner in the country. Then, when asked to do so, this computer can spit out the names and addresses of all the owners of a certain type of car living in a specific section of any city in the nation. Other computers keep inventories for large companies. As something is removed from a warehouse, the computer makes a note of it and, if appropriate, begins the process of reordering.

Other computers help produce newspapers, cars, clothing, and many other things that we use daily. Some computers have the capacity to "call up" quickly every story about a given subject that has ever appeared in a particular newspaper. The government has computers that can summon the names of all persons receiving Social Security checks. Some grocery stores are using computers at their checkout counters which read a label on a grocery item, then tell the cash registers how much to charge, providing the consumers with sales slips showing the amount of each purchase and what was bought. Computers can sort through mountains of information and produce answers that once would have taken humans days—or years—to process.

But as marvelous and unbelievable as these new computers are, they are no match for the Lord our God, the Maker and Redeemer of our universe. God knows everything. He knows everything every computer knows, plus much, much more. There is nothing that God does not know. He knows what is happening now. He knows what has happened. He knows what will happen. God knows it all.

Man's machines and computers, his universities and books, contain far more information than any one person can comprehend. The work that is being done today in biology, in astronomy, in chemistry, boggles the mind. But if man can do all this, why should we be amazed at the ability of God to know all things? For God is the One who gave man the intelligence to build the computer. God gave man the intelligence to understand biology, chemistry, and astronomy. God is the Source of all knowledge.

More than just facts, God knows the thoughts and intentions of all of our hearts and our minds. Everything is openly displayed before God about every creature in the world. By "every creature," I mean not just people, but every living thing. God knows everything there is to know about every butterfly, every insect, every mockingbird, every living creature. "All things are naked" before His eyes (Heb. 4:13).

Jesus said that not even a sparrow falls to the ground without the Father's knowledge (Matt. 10:29). He reminded us that God knows even the number of hairs on our heads (Matt. 10:30). The teaching about the little sparrows is usually interpreted to mean that God is aware when every little sparrow in the world falls to the ground and dies. This is only part of what Jesus meant. Much more is intended in our Lord's teaching about the death of sparrows. The expression "fall on the ground" means "hops on the ground" in the original Greek. God is not only aware when a little bird dies. He also is aware of each little "hop, hop, hop" that every bird makes.

Just think: God knows about each movement of every little sparrow. There are millions of sparrows in the world. There are also many other types of birds—starlings, bluejays, blackbirds, ravens, whooping cranes, etc. And birds are only one part of God's creation. Add to the number of birds that now exist all the billions and trillions of other creatures that exist now on the land, sea, and in the air, and all the creatures that have ever existed and will exist. God knows and cares for each little creature that will ever breathe, or has already breathed its last. If you can even begin to comprehend God's ability to know about all these creatures, you have only begun to understand the width and breadth of the mind and omniscience of God.

Not only does God know all creatures but all things as well (see Heb. 4:13). Every star, every snowflake, every leaf, every blade of grass, every molecule, every action committed by every man, woman, and child, is known to God. At any second of time, God is cognizant of everything that is, was, and shall be, and of how it all relates to everything else. The depth and breadth of God's all-knowing mind is unfathomable.

God's Omniscience—Incentive to Holy Living

God, who knows each hop of a sparrow, also knows our every thought and action as well. Nothing escapes the mind of God. The intentions of our hearts are all an open book before Him. God knows everything there is to know about us.

Few lessons are taught and few sermons are preached on the omniscience of God, the all-knowing nature of God. Perhaps this is because the subject makes us feel so uneasy. Knowing that God sees and knows all that we do, think, and feel fills us with a sense of disquietude. Perhaps we really don't like to think about God knowing the intentions of our hearts, as well as the actions of our lives. But nothing escapes God's glance—absolutely nothing.

What we do is forever written down on the tablet of God's awareness and recorded on the pages of His mind. Just think, God can recall our every action—our highest and most noble actions as well as our lowest and most sinful. The Bible says, "The Spirit of the Lord fell upon me, and said unto me, 'Speak: Thus saith the Lord; Thus have ye said, O house of Israel; for I know the things that come into your mind, every one of them'" (Ezek. 11:5). This verse may frighten us. It may embarrass us. Whatever it does, it is true. God knows everything there is to know. There is no dark dungeon to which we can flee where God does not see us. There is no remote island where we can hide from God. The Scriptures say, "If I make my bed in hell, behold, Thou art there" (Ps. 139:8). If I take wings and fly like the morning, still God knows. If we travel on a spaceship far from the earth, God is aware. No curtain can be stretched so tightly that God cannot see behind it. No deal is made, no decision is ever made that God does not record. No act is committed that God does not see. Nothing escapes the eye of God.

No human saw Cain slay Abel, but God saw, and God acted on what He viewed. God asked Cain for an accounting of what he had done (Gen. 4:8-16).

When Sarah laughed at God's promise, she laughed in her heart and denied her response, but the angel of the Lord knew what human ear had never heard and responded, "Nay, but thou didst laugh" (Gen. 18:15).

No one else knew of Achan's secret sin (Josh. 7), but God knew. The mills of God grind slowly but they grind exceedingly small. The Bible does not say your sins will be found out by other people—for human beings may never know what you have done. Your mother and father may not know. Your spouse may not know. Your employer may not know. Your children may not know. Your neighbor may not know. But God knows. The Bible says, "Be sure your sin will find you out" (Num. 32:23). When our consciences bother us, the sparkle and glow leave our faces, our hearts are disturbed, our steps become unsure. But God knows, and we know. Our sins find us out because He knows all things. "Thou hast set our iniquities before Thee, our secret sins in the light of Thy countenance" (Ps. 90:8).

Omniscience—Encouragement to Our Souls

Instead of being frightened by God's omniscience, we should be grateful and encouraged by it. The fact that God knows everything there is to know about us should fill us with comfort. David said, "Thou knewest my path" (Ps. 142:3). He also said, "Though I walk through the valley of the shadow of death . . . Thou art with me" (Ps. 23:4). God knows when we hurt. He knows the desires of our hearts. He knows who we are and where we should be. God knows the godly and He knows how to deliver them out of temptations. He knows the way through the wilderness of life, even when we have lost our way. God knows the evil that is in us, but he also knows the good. He knows our intentions to do good and our intentions to do evil.

At the same time that God knows all there is to know about us, He also cares for us. He is not a high priest who cannot be touched with feelings about our troubles and infirmities. He not only knows, but He loves us. God cries when we cry. He rejoices when we rejoice. He is not only with us in our sorrow and need; He is ahead of us, unspeakably desirous of answering our pleas and helping us. Isaiah tells us that God says, "And it shall come to pass, that before they call, I will answer, and while they are yet speaking, I will hear" (Isa. 65:24). The Holy Spirit is our constant Companion. The Holy Spirit is that part of God that dwells in the hearts of Christians and reaches out in love to the hearts of non-Christians. The Holy Spirit makes intercession for us with groanings that cannot be uttered. This third Person of the Trinity knows. He cares. He waits to help us with His power. To the suffering church at Smyrna, Jesus Christ said, "I know" (Rev. 2:9).

Jesus confronted Satan for 40 days in a desert (Matt. 4). Three times during that experience, Jesus resisted the overtures of Satan to side with him. Then, on the cross, Jesus utterly defeated Satan. Jesus knows what it is like to suffer and to die. He knows what it is like to be a human being.

So when we say that "God knows," we mean two things: (a) God in Christ knows suffering and death, and (b) God in the Holy Spirit knows what each person today endures. Even more than an inducement to righteous living, the fact that "God knows" should provide the encouragement we need in our times of distress.

God May Be Trusted with the Affairs of Our Lives

It is quite possible that mankind in its original state in paradise knew all things, for Adam and Eve were made in the image of God (Gen. 1:27). But mankind today certainly does not know everything. Even collectively, there is much that we do not know. If we took every fact that is contained in every computer and every fact that is in every book and every fact that is known by every person and combined them all together, it would amount to only a small particle of knowledge in comparison with what God knows. God knows so much more than humans can ever fathom. Our limited knowledge is a direct result of sin. Because of sin, every human being since Adam has been made in the image of man and needs to be remade in the image of God. Because of our sin, we cannot know in the way that God knows.

In our glorified state in heaven, we may again enjoy perfect knowledge. But in this earthly life, complete knowledge is impossible. Wise though some human beings are, we still sadly lack knowledge, compared with the knowledge of the Lord our God. The difference between our knowledge and God's superior knowledge is as wide as the difference between one grain of sand and all the sand on all the shores and deserts of the world.

Our wisest decision, therefore, is to inquire of God and to seek His counsel. We are never taller than when we are on our knees before God in prayer, seeking Him. No promise of Scripture speaks to this truth more than does Romans 8:28: "We know that all things work together for good to them that love God, to them who are the called according to His purpose." Romans 8 teaches that God has a singular purpose for people—that believers will be conformed to the image of His Son in their ultimate state of glorification. "All things"—yes, all things—work together toward that purpose.

God alone knows how much of what to mix together to make a beautiful recipe for our lives. Try for a moment to picture God as the great Chef, putting together a superb recipe for your life. Picture how that recipe, with the right mixture of ingredients, will make your life happy, peaceful, and worthwhile. God, as the Chef, knows how much salt and soda to mix with just the right amount of other ingredients to make a beautiful recipe. But without God as your Master Chef, the recipe for your life will not turn out beautifully.

God's perfect knowledge is available to all believers who will seek it and pray. It is tragic that so few Christians avail themselves of the wisdom that is theirs, just by asking the great Chef of our lives.

Another lesson we must not forget is this: God does not forget. Nothing is hidden from Him or overlooked by Him. Nothing is ever lost to His memory; His knowledge is complete and perfect. God never makes a mistake. He never has a second thought. He never experiences a gap in His memory. He never "blanks out" as we often do. Even the best computers can experience a "stall" or a "down time." But God never has a stall or a down time. God never has to change His mind or catch up. He never receives a new revelation or seeks advice or counsel from others. God's knowledge is as complete as His power is irresistible.

When discussing God's omniscience, we must never forget His perfection. When God acts in the affairs of His children, we can always be sure that He acts on the basis of all knowledge and that He acts in love. His actions are perfect.

God Desires to Impart His Wisdom to Us

The Bible repeatedly presents God as the all-knowing Being who wants us to know His will more than we want to know it. God's knowledge is not a secret thing. He wants to share it with us. God once asked, "Shall I hide from Abraham that thing which I do?" (Gen. 18:17), before He told Abraham what would befall Sodom and Gomorrah.

God's invitation is always open to us. God says, "Call unto Me, and I will answer thee, and show thee great and mighty things, which thou knowest not" (Jer. 33:3). Later the Lord

Jesus added, "Everyone that asketh receiveth; and he that seeketh findeth; and to him that knocketh, it shall be opened" (Luke 11:10).

God is so interested in us that He not only opens His arms to us, but He also pursues us. "For God so loved the world, that He gave His only begotten Son, that whosoever believeth in Him should not perish, but have everlasting life" (John 3:16). In this familiar verse, we are told that God wanted us for His own so badly that He sent the ultimate Gift—His very own Son—to offer us abundant life.

So the key question is, How can we as individuals know the will of God? If God knows everything and is willing to share Himself with us, how can we get in tune with His will for our lives?

First, we must be sure we understand that God is anxious for us to know Him. He is not hiding behind a tree or under a rock. He is not playing cat and mouse. He wants to talk with us. He wants to reveal His truths to us. And His only qualifications are that we know Him and that we seek His face.

God is waiting to hear your voice. He yearns for you to call. You may not know the exact words to say, but God is willing to listen to your prayer. No child's prayer goes unanswered. No young person is ever turned away. God hurts when we hurt. God wants to answer prayer. He wants to help you, if only you will ask Him.

Even though God knows all there is to know about us, He still loves us. His omniscience does not separate us from Him. It draws Him closer to us. Eternity alone will reveal the massive mistakes, the lost time, the needless and tragic follies that each of us has made because we did not always seek His counsel. But eternity also will reveal when we turned to Him, trusted Him, and put our faith in Him. In His omniscience, God knows the desires—both good and evil—of our lives. He knows when we want to seek Him. He knows when our souls cry out to Him. He knows when there is the slightest, stumbling, bumbling impulse toward letting Him become Lord of our lives, Ruler of our souls, and Master of our efforts.

His Plan for Our Lives Is Based on His Foreknowledge

Those who believe on God's Son as their Lord and Saviour are saved from their sins. That's the message, the Good News, of the Bible. And if we are saved, we shall live with God in heaven. The final glorification of a believer—our finished state in heaven—will be to "be like Him, for we shall see Him as He is" (1 John 3:2). This final state will be based on both justification and predestination. And on what does this great doctrine of God's predestination rest? On nothing less than on the immutable rock of His foreknowledge, on His omniscience. "For whom He did foreknow, He also did predestinate to be conformed to the image of His Son, that He might be the firstborn among many brethren" (Rom. 8:29). What God decides beforehand to do, on the basis of His all-inclusive knowledge, He does. Nothing can interrupt the process, from foreknowledge to glorification. God, having foreknown me, did predestine me to be conformed to the image of His Son. And nothing—but nothing—shall separate true believers from the final accomplishment of that fact.

If God, on the basis of His perfect knowledge, predetermines my ultimate glorification, when I shall know all things, does it not follow that the intervening process between foreknowledge and glorification should be lived on the basis of that knowledge?

Author Francis Schaeffer has asked an important question in the title to one of his many books: *How Shall We Then Live?* Indeed, that is the question we must ask in this discussion of God's omniscience. Wherein shall we live in this earthly journey between foreknowledge before the worlds began, and glorification (including perfect knowledge) after the world shall end and eternity begin? The answer is available to all of us. It is found in God's perfect knowledge, which is free to each Christian who will pray and ask Him for it. "Ask, and ye shall receive, that your joy may be full" (John 16:24).

8
God Is
Ever-Present

Whither shall I go from Thy Spirit? Or whither shall I flee from Thy presence? If I ascend up into heaven, Thou art there. If I make my bed in hell, behold, Thou art there. If I take the wings of the morning, and dwell in the uttermost parts of the sea; even there shall Thy hand lead me, and Thy right hand shall hold me. If I say, "Surely the darkness shall cover me; even the night shall be light about me," yea, the darkness hideth not from Thee, but the night shineth as the day; the darkness and the light are both alike to Thee. Psalm 139:7-12

"Where is God?" a small child asks. Pointing his small, chubby hand to the heavens, he again wants to know: "Does God live up there?"

Those are not only the questions of a child. They are the questions of many men and women today. "Where is God?" people ask when they want to seek Him. Others ask, "Where is God?" in order to deny His existence. They ask the question with a sneer, secretly believing that no one can answer their question.

Where is God? The question is asked as if there can be only one answer. We want someone to answer the question by pointing to a specific place and saying that there is where God makes His home. We cannot, however, point to just one location and call that the only dwelling place for God, the only place where a person may find God. The God we worship is not just in one place, for He is everywhere at once. He is not just in the highest heaven or in the lowest hell. He is not just on the tallest mountain or in the deepest ravine. The Lord our God is everywhere at once.

Where is God? Every Christian may respond, "In my heart." This is a correct answer. But it is only part of the answer. Where is God? He is everywhere. God is in the hearts of all believers. God is in the heavens above. God is wherever a nonbeliever gropes for the answers to the universe. God is everywhere. We must never try to limit Him to any one place.

Theologians have a fancy word to describe this characteristic of God. The word in omnipresence. The term is not found in our Bibles. However, it graphically describes one characteristic about God that is described in detail in our Bibles. Omnipresence simply means that God is everywhere at once.

It is impossible for us to comprehend how anyone or anything can be in even two places at the same time. In our human minds, we think that if something is in one place it cannot be somewhere else at the same time. But God defies this method of reasoning. God is everywhere at once. The fact that finite man is not equipped mentally to comprehend a concept does not negate its reality. Just because we cannot fully grasp how God can be in many places at the same time does not mean that it is not true.

In your home, there are pictures you cannot see and sounds you cannot hear. These pictures are being broadcast over television waves. These sounds are being broadcast over radio waves. You cannot see these television and radio waves with just your naked eyes. You cannot hear the radio waves with your unaided ears. Without a television set these television waves cannot be received, let alone understood or viewed. Without a radio, radio waves cannot be received or heard. But the fact that you are unable to see what is on the television waves with your naked eye without a television receiver does not make these TV waves nonexistent. The fact that you are unable to comprehend them takes nothing away from their existence. The problem is simply that you don't have the right equipment to receive their messages. By using a television set or a radio, these sounds and pictures may be experienced—if you wish. But with or without your capacity to receive these messages, they still exist.

Do you see my point? Perhaps in heaven we will have "glorified receivers" which will make it possible for us to understand things that pass us by in our present existence. We do not yet have these "glorified receivers," and the doctrine of God's omnipresence may not fully be comprehended by earthlings yet. The nature of God is that He who is within us can be at once above and beyond us.

Omnipresence Is in Evidence in the Trinity

One of the clearest evidences of God's omnipresence is in the Trinity. Many people misunderstand the Trinity. They assume that we Christians worship three Gods—Father, Son, and Holy Spirit. Those who think this express a profound misunderstanding of the Trinity and what we Christians believe.

Our God is one God. He is not three Gods. God is one God, yet is also Three in One. God is present in three different forms, but they are all Three the same God. The fact that our God can be one God, yet Three in One, is beyond human comprehension. St. Augustine said, "Blessed is the man that accepts spiritual mysteries without having to understand them."

Jesus referred to Himself, the Holy Spirit, and the Father

interchangeably. "Let not your heart be troubled," Jesus said, "ye believe in God, believe also in Me" (John 14:1). A bit later Jesus said, "I am the way, the truth, and the life; no man cometh unto the Father, but by Me" (John 14:6). Then Jesus added, "I am in the Father; and the Father in Me" (John 14:11).

To a nonbeliever these words may sound like nonsense, or like utter confusion. But they are neither. These words of Jesus speak eternal truths about the relationship of God the Father and God the Son.

In essence, the coming of the Holy Spirit was the return of Christ in an invisible form, rather than in an earthly body. Jesus taught that the world would never accept this doctrine because it accepts only what it can see (John 14:17). Jesus promised to send the Comforter, the Holy Spirit. And what would happen when the Holy Spirit came? "I will come to you," said Jesus (John 14:18). Note the use of the word "I." Jesus was identifying Himself with the Comforter, yet He was speaking of the Comforter as a separate Person. Just as the Father was in Jesus, so the Holy Spirit was in Jesus. And just as the Father was in the Holy Spirit, so was the Son in the Holy Spirit. Remember the words of Jesus: "The words that I speak unto you I speak not of Myself; but the Father that dwelleth in Me" (John 14:10).

Jesus clearly taught that the Father, Son, and Holy Spirit are interchangeable expressions of one true God. Our God can indeed be in more than one form. Not only that, He can be everywhere at once.

When God is in heaven running the mighty universe, He exists as the Father; when He expresses Himself in love and judgment to the world, He acts as the Son. Remember these words of Jesus: "For the Father judgeth no man, but hath committed all judgment unto the Son" (John 5:22). When God is in the invisible form in the world drawing people to Himself and indwelling believers, He acts as the Holy Spirit. It is the same God, only in three different expressions.

No Form of God Is Greater than Another

There are no stairsteps of authority in the Trinity. Some people think of Jesus as God's little boy and the Holy Spirit as God's errand boy. This is far from the truth. When Jesus was born in a stable and laid in a manger, He was also mighty God. Though the Holy Spirit indwells our hearts, He is also mighty God.

God the Father, God the Son, and God the Holy Spirit are all One and They are all equal. We should not refer to the Trinity as "God, Jesus, and the Holy Spirit." Instead we should call Them, "God the Father, God the Son, and God the Holy Spirit." It is never "God and the other Two." We worship one God in three forms. Regardless of the form, regardless of the place, regardless of the action, God is one and He can be everywhere at once.

Does this concept seem awesome to you? Indeed, it should. God's greatness is more than we mortals can ever fully comprehend. The most important fact for us to remember is that God is with us wherever we may go. From the first moment of my conception until my last breath God is with me. In childhood He was protecting me, preserving me; in young manhood, convicting me, drawing me to Christ; indwelling and empowering me since I have received Him into my life. God is always there.

Isn't that comforting to know? There is no place that we can hide from God. There is no place in the world where God is absent. There is within each of us a childlike instinct to want to find somewhere where we can hide from God. But we cannot. God is always with us. God may come to us in different forms, but He is the same God—all-powerful, all-knowing, and all-present.

Omnipresence Is Not Pantheism

Some ancients were pantheists, believing that there were gods in everything. To them, gods inhabited individual trees, stones, and even items made by other men. This concept is entirely different from what we mean when we say God is everywhere at once. Pantheism perverts omnipresence to mean that nature, in which God indwells, becomes God too. This is not what Christians mean when we say God in omnipresent. God is in everything; indeed He created everything. But that does not mean that we should worship everything. To a believer in pantheism, all nature should be worshiped. So if God is in a pencil, the pencil is worshiped, for the pencil is God. If God indwells nature, nature should be praised, for it has become God and is, therefore, the object of our worship.

Pantheism confuses the created with the Creator. It substitutes the complex for the simple, and in so doing entirely perverts and distorts the concept of the omnipresent God.

As Christians, we believe that while God is not excluded from anything, neither is He totally contained in created objects, even the sum of His creation. Jesus Christ is totally God, and in Him all the fullness of the Godhead dwells bodily. But the Father was no less God when the Son was on earth. God is no less God when He indwells a believer than is the Holy Spirit. That God may be in man or in nature is no reason to worship man or nature as God.

Jesus Christ was the complete revelation of God in terms of human understanding, and was God's full revelation of Himself. Yet the Father was no less God when He indwelt the Son.

One of the earliest Christian heresies was a theology called montanism. This doctrine perverted the concept of the Trinity, because it tried to reduce this great mystery into a pattern that conforms with human understanding. According to this belief, God was present in three forms, but not at the same time. In other words, God became the Father, then the Son, finally

the Holy Spirit. To the montanists, God was not simultaneously God the Father, God the Son, and God the Holy Spirit. He
was the God who *became* the Father and then the Son and
then the Holy Spirit. The difference is important for our understanding here. Montanists could not speak of God as existing in three forms at the same time.

This misunderstanding of God's ability to transcend time,
space, and form was also evident in the so-called "God is
Dead" theologies of the 1960s. Remember that movement? On
the cover of a *Time* magazine was the imposing question, "Is
God Dead?" Several so-called theologians spoke of the death of
God as if somehow God could die. They talked about how God
had changed forms and the God we Christians perceived had
died and taken on a newer, more transcendent form.

This, as you know, was a false theology. God has not died.
Nor has He given up or died to one form to take on a newer
form. God is the same yesterday, today, tomorrow, and forever. He does not take on one form, to discard it later for
another, as one dons and then removes a Halloween mask.
Our God is consistently the same.

Now, back to the point about pantheism: God does not take
on the form of nature, so that we should worship trees, mountains, and animals. Trees and mountains are not God, though
God is in everything including trees and mountains. Inani-
mate nature knows nothing of an expression of love, mercy,
and holiness. Mountains, trees, and animals all point to the
majesty and grandeur of God, but they are not God. They are
God's handiwork.

The only living incarnation of God is in the Son and in the
continuing incarnation of His body, the church on earth, fitly
joined by the Spirit to its Head in heaven. Only Christ expresses
the fullness of the Godhead bodily. Any other manifestation is
less than a complete expression of His fullness. Let God alone
be praised! Let God alone be worshiped!

Metaphysics and the Omnipresent God

There are other misunderstandings of the omnipresence of God. Among these is that advocated by metaphysics.

That God is everywhere at once must not be misunderstood to rob God of His human personality in Jesus Christ. Christian Science, a metaphysical religion, teaches that "the Second Coming of Christ" is to be understood in terms of Christ's coming to us repeatedly through new truth which is given through teachers. But no such mystical abstraction will suffice to define either Christ's personal incarnation or His personal presence with us.

By omnipresence, we do not mean mystical abstraction. God is a personality with mind, emotion, and will. He knows things, He feels things, and He does things. God is not limited to the mystique of His Creation. As Author and Consummator of all that is, God holds the worlds in His hands and is not restricted to an expression of Himself through the dimensions of its mysteries. He is divine Being and supreme Personality. But His divinity and supremacy must not stand beyond His personality. He is not something; He is Somebody. That is a major difference. The ultimate Personage, yes; but personality nonetheless, who has adequately expressed Himself in the person of Jesus Christ, for "in Him dwelleth all the fullness of the Godhead bodily" (Col. 2:9).

God's Omnipresence Does Not Diminish His Intimacy

God is not only in heaven running His mighty universe. He is also still "a Friend that sticketh closer than a brother" (Prov. 18:24). Nothing escapes God's all-knowing gaze, His all-caring compassion, and His all-present empathy. He is not a mere observer but an ever-present Help in times of trouble (Ps. 46:1).

Some theologians and philosophers debate about the personal nature of God. They ask each other: "Is God *both* immanent and transcendent? Or is He one or the other?" By immanent, they mean that God is close at hand, in this world and in our hearts. By transcendent, they mean that God is beyond this world and beyond our realm of understanding. Some theologians and philosophers argue that God is only transcendent, or other-worldly. They cannot conceive of God as close at hand. They picture God as having created the universe and then set it loose to operate on its own, apart from Him. Others say God is immanent, or nearby. These theologians argue that God is as near as the "still small voice" (1 Kings 19:12) inside of us.

The correct view of God is that He is both transcendent and immanent. God is both beyond this world and also integrally intertwined in it. God is everywhere—in our hearts, in our world, as well as in heaven.

God is not only present in our world, but He is also intimately involved in and acquainted with the lives of His children. So real is His intimate relationship with His children that the Apostle Paul said to join our bodies to that of a harlot is to bring Him into an adulterous relationship (1 Cor. 6:16). "What? Know ye not that your body is the temple of the Holy Ghost which is in you?" (1 Cor. 6:19)

In one sense, God has no hands but my hands, no eyes but my eyes, no lips but my lips. Where I go, I take Christ with me. Paul said, "Christ liveth in me, and the life which I now live in the flesh I live by the faith of the Son of God, who loved me, and gave Himself for me" (Gal. 2:20). This means that Christ literally goes with us believers wherever we go, for He is deeply imbedded in our hearts. When I need Him, He is always there. God not only cares for me, but He resides within me as a sensitive Presence, an unseen Guest at every meal, a silent Participant in every act.

It is difficult for some people to understand and accept

God's immanence and His transcendence. Only if we believe fully in His omnipresence can we accept these seemingly contradictory ways of God's existing. God is not only "out there," but He is also "in here." God knows every fact about this great universe, and He also knows every secret hidden in our hearts.

We should be grateful that we cannot escape God's presence, for He comes to us not only in judgment but also in forgiveness and love.

God's Omnipresence Will Be Magnified in Heaven

As real as God seems to us now, He will be even more real when our faith gives way to actual sight. When we see Him face to face, we will see the tender compassion of the One who led us all the way.

> In shady green pastures, so rich and so sweet,
> God leads His dear children along.
> Where the water's cool flow bathes the weary one's feet,
> God leads His dear children along.
> Some through the waters, some through the flood,
> Some through the fire, but all through the blood;
> Some through great sorrow, but God gives a song,
> In the night season and all the day long.
> —G. A. Young

Only in heaven will we fully understand God and His glory and His power. Only eternity will reveal the full manifestation of His presence to us. And what a glorious unveiling it will be!

We may think we understand God now. But we have only begun to understand Him. God is so much more than we can ever imagine in this life. For in this life, we "see through a glass, darkly" (1 Cor. 13:12) but in heaven we shall see plainly. From this world, we can only guess at the magnificent beauty of our Lord. We can only guess at the meaning behind all that God does for us in this life.

But the day will come when we will live with God, and then we shall know His glory and be able to fully understand His omnipresence. When we are with God we will understand how He can rule in heaven and also reign within the heart of every obedient believer.

The story is told of a weary Christian who had a dream. In his dream, he saw two sets of footprints walking along the sand. Suddenly he noticed that several yards back one set disappeared and only one set continued. When this Christian met the Lord in heaven he complained that Christ had been untrue to His promise to walk with him all the way and had obviously, somehow, forsaken him in his need.

"No," replied the Lord. "Where the two sets of prints became one is the point at which you walked through deep valleys. The reason there was only one set of footprints from that point forward is because then I began carrying you."

That's the way it will be for all Christians when we get to heaven. The things of this world that we do not understand now will be explained to us then. And when we are with God in heaven we will understand how He not only dwelled in our hearts, but also how He literally carried each of us through the deep valleys of our lives.

In this life, it is hard to understand the nature of God. It is especially difficult to understand how God can be everywhere at the same time, yet be the Ruler over heaven and earth as well as God the Father, God the Son, and God the Holy Spirit. But in heaven, thank the dear Lord, we shall understand fully.

9
God Is
All-Powerful

And I heard as it were the voice of a great multitude, and as the voice of many waters, and as the voice of mighty thunderings, saying, "Alleluia: for the Lord God omnipotent reigneth."

Revelation 19:6

The Lord our God is not just powerful; He is *all*-powerful. This means He has all power. Just think: God controls all the power in the universe. He is the Source of all power.

There is a fancy theological word that describes this characteristic of God. That word is omnipotent. The term is actually a conjugation of two words, *omni* meaning all, and *potence* meaning power. The word omnipotent is used only one time in our Bible, in Revelation 19:6. Our heavenly Father is described in that verse as "the Lord God omnipotent." Literally, this means "the Lord God who is all-powerful."

So what does it mean when we say God is all-powerful? It means much more than we may be willing to admit. We know that God is sovereign, that He has the right to do as He chooses, as He wills. The question then arises, "Does God have the strength to support that sovereignty?" Another way to phrase that question is: "Is God big enough to back up what He says and what He wills?" The answer to both questions is, "Yes, a thousand times yes." Yes, God has the strength to support His sovereignty. Yes, God has the power to back up what He says and what He wills. If God does not have the power to back up His sovereignty and His authority, then He is not capable of being God. But if God is sovereign, then it is essential that He also be omnipotent.

The seals of the 50 states in America carry such words as "The Sovereign State of Missouri" and "The Sovereign State of Ohio." Used in this context, the word sovereign means the authority to make laws and the accompanying power and responsibility to enforce those laws.

The Lord our God is sovereign also. But He is much more sovereign than are any of the 50 states in America. He is much more powerful than the whole of the United States of America. He is much more powerful than all of the nations of the earth put together. God is more powerful than all the governments combined that have ever existed and all those that ever will exist. God is more powerful than all the people combined who have ever lived, plus all those who will live. God *is* sovereign, and as such, He *is* all-powerful.

No Power Is Greater than God's

Just as no person can stand against God's sovereignty, so none can stand against His power. There is no one on earth or in heaven or in hell who is as powerful as God. Lucifer wanted to be like God in power, but he was cast out of heaven by the more powerful God. No one can compete against God's omnipotence and will. God's power always wins out in the end.

God's power is greater even than the laws of the universe, which He established. In performing a miracle, for example, God does not set aside the natural law He Himself has established. He simply superimposes upon that law the higher law of His omnipotence. God's omnipotence is greater than any natural law. Unbelievers may ask, "How could God make the sun stand still in the sky?" Or, "How could God cause a virgin to conceive?" A believer doesn't ask such questions, because he or she knows that God is so powerful that He can cause anything to happen that He wills.

Jesus said, "All power is given unto Me in heaven and in earth" (Matt. 28:18). Jesus had that power because He is also God. While God may choose to impose heavenly power upon earthly power, it is all *His* power, even in the divine performance of the miraculous. What God wills to do, He does. Nothing can stand against God's power—not even the natural laws that He has created.

Anyone who has less power than God is not God. He who is incapable of performing all of his own good pleasure is less than God. We humans are not God, for we have no power except what God gives us. Satan is not God, for he will someday be required to answer to God's power. Angels are not God, for their power too comes only from God.

In His sovereignty, God tells His subjects to be holy (1 Peter 1:15-16). But when His subjects sin, God in love provides righteousness for us so that we can stand "accepted in the beloved" (Eph. 1:6). This is all operative because of God's power. God has the power to judge us unworthy, and He has the power to make up for our unworthiness.

The power of God includes His ability to bring about the holiness He has willed for His creations. Without power, the mercy and love of God would be no more than feeble pity. Without power, the promises of God would only be empty sounds. Without power, the threatening of God's judgments would be like a scarecrow in a field that looked frightening, but had no strength at all to enforce any authority over the field.

All Power Belongs to God

All power belongs to God because of who He is. God's power is eternal, infinite, incomprehensible. His omnipotence comes not by man's decree, or even by God's own decision. His omnipotence is not given by any heavenly tribunal or decreed by a celestial court. The power of God is intrinsic in His nature. It is His, of and within Himself.

So God's power cannot be restrained, checked, withstood, or frustrated by His creatures. No power on earth can match that of God. This truth about God's omnipotence was profoundly etched on David's heart. He inscribed his impression of it: "God hath spoken once; twice have I heard this; that power belongeth unto God" (Ps. 62:11).

Our God, who is the same yesterday, today, and forever, is also all-powerful in the past, in the present, and in the future. Here is how David, in another psalm, described God's power: "The Lord also thundered in the heavens, and the Highest gave His voice: hailstones and coals of fire. Yea, He sent out His arrows, and scattered them; and He shot out lightnings and discomfited them. Then the channels of waters were seen, and the foundations of the world were discovered at Thy rebuke, O Lord, at the blast of the breath of Thy nostrils" (Ps. 18:13-15).

God's power was in evidence at the creation of our world. It is present today in the redemption God offers to all of us. It will be present in the future when He judges His world.

Compared with God's power, our human power is nothing. Compared with God, the human race is powerless. The world is powerless compared with God. Satan is powerless compared with God. There is nothing that can equal God's power. Daniel expressed this idea beautifully: "All the inhabitants of the earth are reputed as nothing; and He doeth according to His will in the army of heaven, and among the inhabitants of the earth: and none can stay His hand, or say unto Him, 'What doest Thou?'" (Dan. 4:35)

God Rules Because He Can Enforce His Will

God has the authority to rule the earth, and He has the accompanying power to enforce His will. God is accountable to no one; He answers to no court; He bows before no man. The sovereign nature of God's authority and His power stand unchallenged. Death cannot challenge God, for He is eternal.

There is no decision that can be made anywhere in the universe or in heaven that can rebuke God. Satan's power is insignificant compared with God's power. The kings of earth rule only by the grace of God; they have no power of their own.

God's acts in Creation illustrate His power. To the earth, the stars, the planets, and the whole universe, God said, "Be," and they were.

To the seas, He said, "Bring forth the fish." To each living thing, God said, "Bring forth" after your own "kind" (Gen. 1).

> To the winds, God said, "Blow."
> To the seas, He said, "Divide."
> To the Red Sea, He said, "Part."
> To Lazarus, Jesus said, "Come forth."
> To demons, He said, "Come ye out of him."
> To the storm, He said, "Be still."
> To Satan, He said, "Get thee behind Me."

And in each case, what God said came to pass. The seas brought forth fish. Living animals reproduced. The winds blew. The seas divided. The Red Sea parted for Moses. Lazarus came forth from his grave. The demons fled at Jesus' instruction. The storms fell silent for Jesus. Satan fled from Jesus.

Some television ads claim that whenever a certain stockbroker speaks, people listen. These commercials might be compared with what it is like when God speaks. We should listen, because God's words contain much more power than anyone else's.

All Earthly Power Comes from God

The power of God is the only real power there is. There is no power apart from God. God's power created the universe. God's power keeps it going. We mortals have no power except that which was given to us at Creation. Satan has no power of his own, but only that which is temporarily granted to him through God's permissive will. Satan must come before the throne of God, as he did with Job, for permission to make even the most insignificant of decisions. God will not allow Satan to test any human being beyond the sovereign limits of His will. And even then, God will give that person a power greater than Satan's, and with the temptation, provide a way of escape that he may be able to bear it (1 Cor. 10:13). Satan has no power at all, except as God wills it.

The greatest power in the world today is that which God has given His people through Pentecost. In the Upper Room, God breathed His Holy Spirit on His church. The church has no power except that which God has given it. When early believers went forth to witness to the world about the death and resurrection of Jesus and God's love, God gave them the spiritual power they needed to testify and preach and carry His Word so that others might hear it and receive Him.

Jesus said, "All power is given unto Me in heaven and in earth" (Matt. 28:18). Earlier He had prayed, "For Thine is the kingdom, and the power, and the glory, forever" (Matt. 6:13). Jesus knew that all spiritual power—yea, all power—comes from God. And since He is God, He knew He had all power too.

The power of Jesus is nowhere more evident than at the conversion of a lost man or woman, boy or girl. As Paul said, "The life which I now live in the flesh I live by the faith of the Son of God, who loved me and gave Himself for me" (Gal. 2:20).

The Holy Spirit is directly involved in each conversion experience. At conversion, Jesus Christ comes to reside in a person's heart. Jesus is literally born into one's being. Christ now lives in His newborn child. Note that Paul did not say, "I live this present life by my faith in the Son of God." Instead, he said, "I live by the faith *of* the Son of God." We do not live our earthly lives by faith in a distant, remote God who is beyond us, but by the power of a Christ who is both incarnate God and incarnate *within* us. In the new birth, Jesus Christ brings all that God is into all that we are. The new birth means that God begins to live within us. His authority, His holiness, His power—all of His attributes—are positionally ours and become experientially enlarged as we daily mature in Him. The power that we know as believers, then, is not our power, but it is God's power operating through our personalities. God gives us power to love, to witness, to serve, to stand against the evil that fills our world. As we depend on Christ, our lives literally become lived "by the faith of the Son of God."

We Mortals Have No Power of Our Own

I have no power that is my own. The greatest Christians who ever walked this earth had no power of their own. Satan has no power of his own. The universe has no inherent power to sustain itself. All things were made by Christ, all things consist in Him, and He upholds them.

We must get a firm grasp of what Jesus meant when He said, "All power [authority] is given unto Me" (Matt. 28:18). The only power that exists anywhere in the world is power allowed by God within His permissive or perfect will. There is no power unless God wills or allows it. And because Jesus is God as well as man, He too is the source of all the power in the universe.

Look at it another way. All the power—physical and spiritual—that we have in this world is borrowed from God. Man's borrowed power can add nothing to God's great power because it was all God's in the first place. We are literally in debt to God for whatever power we possess in this world.

As the song says, "He's got the whole world in His hands." God sits on His throne supported by no assisting arm. No one undergirds God's power. God is attended by no courtier and borrows no splendor from His creatures. Remember what God said to Job?

> Where wast thou when I laid the foundations of the earth?
> Declare, if thou hast understanding.
> Who hath laid the measures thereof, if thou knowest?
> Or who hath stretched the line upon it?
> Whereupon are the foundations thereof fastened.
> Or who laid the cornerstone thereof? (Job 38:4-6)

A psalmist wrote, "It is He that hath made us, and not we ourselves. We are His people, and the sheep of His pasture" (Ps. 100:3). All authority and power belong to God. We too belong to Him. Thus Jesus could say, "In the world ye shall have tribulation; but be of good cheer; I have overcome the world" (John 16:33). The Apostle John added, "Greater is He that is in you than he that is in the world" (1 John 4:4).

God Gives Us Spiritual Power

Among the ancients, the position on the right side of a ruler was the position of highest honor. Jesus described Himself as seated at "the right hand of power" (Matt. 26:64).

In ancient Israel, a high priest went into the temple's holy of holies in Jerusalem once a year to make atonement for the sins of the people. Beyond the veil of the holy of holies was no chair, indicating that the high priest could not be seated, for his work was never done. But after Christ died for our sins, His once-for-all sacrifice completed His task, so He sat down at the right hand of God. Jesus is in the seat of authority at the right hand of God. And on what basis? The exclusive basis of His accomplishment at Calvary, the purchasing of our salvation through His own shed blood. It is by His finished work on Calvary that Jesus has the authority to mediate between God and man (1 Tim. 2:5) and to open a channel for redeemed man to know the power of God.

Jesus sent His disciples out to minister in His name. He "began to send them forth by two and two, and gave them power over unclean spirits" (Mark 6:7). The power to minister aright does not come from man's power; it comes from God's power. The power of the Holy Spirit could not come until our Lord ascended back to heaven to intercede with His blood. In the Old Testament era the Spirit of God never came into people, only upon them, anointing them temporarily for service. But when Christ died once for all, the veil of the temple was torn from top to bottom, indicating that the separation between God and man was removed for all time by the finished work of Christ. We who know and obey Christ can, therefore, come boldly before God's throne asking whatever we wish, within His will and in His name (Heb. 4:16; 1 John 5:14-15).

To know God, then, is to have access to His power. Because we are His, we are recipients of His grace and subsequently of His power. Seated at the right hand of power, Jesus is the great Baptizer with the Holy Spirit, through which the power of God is available to people.

We Know Only a Tiny Fraction of God's Power

God's power is evident everywhere in our world and in the lives of His children. But, as greatly as His power has been manifest, we still only know a microscopic part of it all. Job tells us:

> He divided the sea with His power, and by His understanding
> He smiteth through the proud. By His Spirit, He hath garnished

the heavens; His hand hath formed the crooked serpent. Lo,
these are parts of His ways; but how little a portion is heard of
Him? But the thunder of His power, who can understand? (Job
26:12-14)

Job clearly understood that God's power is greater than anything mortals can comprehend. How can anyone underesti-
mate God's power? Dead things are formed under the waters;
Shiloh is naked before Him; He stretched out the empty spot in
the northern skies; He suspends the earth upon nothing; He
stores the waters in the clouds; the pillars of heaven tremble
before Him; He parts the sea with His will; and yet, "These are
parts of His ways," just a little portion of His power.

Job asked, "But the thunder of His power, who can understand?" Job answered himself, saying that even the sound of
the power God makes is so awesome it is incomprehensible.
How could we ever expect to comprehend God's power itself?
"His brightness was as the light. He had horns coming out of
His hand; and there was the hiding of His power" (Hab. 3:4).
Even the magnificent display of God's power in the visions to
the prophets and in the Book of Revelation hid much of His
power.

No full display of God's strength has ever been made to
man. And perhaps it never shall be. But it is enough to say that
"The heavens declare the glory of God, and the firmament
showeth His handiwork" (Ps. 19:1). How can we ever ask
whether God is able? The prayers, the problems, and the
needs of His people are all known to Him and He is able to do
anything, meet any need, change any situation, make any provision, solve any problem. *"All things are possible to him that
believeth"* (Mark 9:23). Since the great things God has done are
just a microscopic part of His mighty power, it behooves us to
pay the price, walk humbly before Him, seek His face, and
strive to find out what He can do through our lives. Here is an

incomprehensible thought: God in a moment could save all the heathen of the world, solve every problem, and change our world to a paradise.

The power is there. Its availability is certain. May the people of God give fresh commitment to the priority of seeking to know His power. He only waits for broken vessels that He may reshape, and empty containers that He may fill. "Lord, as of old at Pentecost, Thou didst Thy power display; with cleansing, purifying flame descend on us today" (Charles H. Gabriel).

Without God's Power, Where Would We Be?

An anonymous but eloquent author has penned words in the style of a southern Gospel preacher:

> I sat alone at the midnight hour and watched the handiwork of God in the deep blue sky. I asked myself this question:
> Without the power of God, who am I?
> Without the power of God, I'm unable to walk, talk, sing, or play.
> Without the power of God, I have no guide to lead me day by day.
> Without the power of God, I have no vigor or vim.
> Without the power of God, I have no activity of my limbs.
> Without the power of God, I'm unable to laugh or cry.
> By the power of God I live or I die.
> Then without the power of God, who am I?
>
> Without the power of God, what is man?
> It is a shame how men will take God's power and use it to a low disgrace.
> They will take His tongue, His lips, His breath and curse Him to His face.
> If God should recall His power to come on high, men everywhere would cease to live.
> Even we would surely die.

10
God Is
Faithful

*God is our refuge and strength, a very present help in trouble.
Therefore will not we fear, though the earth be removed, and
though the mountains be carried into the midst of the sea.*

Psalm 46:1-2

*Be Thou my strong habitation, whereunto I may continually
resort. Thou hast given commandment to save me, for Thou art
my Rock and my Fortress.*

Psalm 71:3

*The children of men put their trust under the shadow of Thy
wings.*

Psalm 36:7

God is our steadfast Anchor amid the storms and stresses in
life, and our future rests securely on His solid foundation. We
can live peaceably in calm assurance, because our God is
faithful to His Word.

What does it mean to say that God is faithful? It means that
what God promises to do, He will do. What He says, He does.
God does not promise one thing today, and change His mind

tomorrow. What He promises today, He will do.

How wonderful it is that we can rely on such a God, who is the same yesterday, today, and tomorrow!

But does God always come through for us in the way that we want Him to? Does God always arrive to rescue us from our problems, as the cavalries in the movies always arrived just as the Indians were about to take the forts?

At first it may sound like a contradiction to say that God is faithful to His Word, but then to add that He does not always do what we ask. But this is no contradiction. If God says He will do something, He does it. But if we ask Him to do something, He answers us in the way that is best for us. His answers are not always our answers.

Paul wrote, "I can do all things through Christ which strengtheneth me" (Phil. 4:13). This does not mean that just because we ask God for something, what we have requested will automatically be ours. God gives us the strength to face up to those moments and times when life is not what we want it to be. But God also gives us the strength to take the bad moments and turn them into better situations. With Christ, we can do all things, and with Christ, all things are possible. But sometimes things are not as we wish them to be. God often has a higher purpose for our lives than we are able to understand.

God is not our servant, answering to our beck and call. This is not what we mean when we say God is faithful. God is faithful to His Word, but He is not a genie in a bottle who will spoil us by granting all our wishes.

God Did Not Spare Job or Others

When we read the Bible, we realize that God did not spare Job, or Daniel, or Paul, or John, or even His own Son from the pain and suffering of this world. Each of these men suffered, as you and I suffer in this life. Was God unfaithful to them? Absolutely not! God was faithful to each of them, though He did not grant their every wish and desire. Do you remember how Jesus prayed on the night before He was crucified? He said, "O My Father, if this cup may not pass away from Me, except I drink it, Thy will be done" (Matt. 26:42). Jesus was saying that His human desire was not to suffer on the cross, but that He was willing to undergo such torment and torture for a greater divine purpose. Jesus could have summoned a legion of angels to rescue Him, but He didn't. He knew that there was a greater purpose in His suffering.

How many times in our own lives have we asked God to get us out of a jam and He did not do it? Are we only supposed to talk about the times God answered us exactly as we have requested? No, of course not. There are times that God does not appear to come through with what we've asked. But that is from our perspective. From God's perspective, the answer is different. God is faithful to His purpose in this world.

In the Book of Daniel, we read that King Nebuchadnezzar set up a great image and commanded his subjects to worship it. Three Hebrew servants of God refused to bow their knees to the idol and were brought before the king to account for themselves. Though threatened with incineration in a fiery furnace, they steadfastly refused to offend God in order to please the king. This is what they said to Nebuchadnezzar:

> If it be so, our God whom we serve is able to deliver us from the burning fiery furnace, and He will deliver us out of thine hand, O king. *But if not,* be it known unto thee, O king, that we will not serve thy gods, nor worship the golden image which thou hast set up (Dan. 3:17-19).

These verses capture the essence of the attitude we need to have about the faithfulness of God. This attitude represents the most wholesome and mature psychological, emotional, and spiritual response I know to the problem of going through the fire without deliverance. Our God is able to deliver us from every trial and trouble. But if He chooses not to do so, we are still going to love Him and serve Him and obey Him! He can deliver us if He wants to, but if He chooses not to, that is His business. God has His reasons for doing as He does, and we need to trust Him whether or not He answers us in the way we want to be answered. With Job, the three young men in the fiery furnace could say, "Though He slay me, yet will I trust in Him!" (Job 13:15)

Learning to rely on the faithfulness of God is a great lesson for all Christians to learn. But it is not an easy lesson to master. It is much easier to moan and groan about our demands that God has not granted, or our whims that He has not fulfilled.

How then do we develop an attitude which places our reliance totally on the faithfulness of God? How is such an attitude possible? I believe there are six factors we need to keep in mind about God which will help us live our lives with trust in the faithfulness of God. These six things give us the framework for our own assurance in Him. The three young Hebrew men knew these six factors about God. We too should remember them and keep them always before us.

God's Love Is Dependable

We should not dwell on whether God has rescued us every time we have gotten ourselves in trouble, but we should focus on His love. I readily admit that God does not always rescue us from every dilemma. He has His reasons, though sometimes we may not understand them. But He has answered our requests enough times to prove that He does love us. Those times that He has rescued us have proven His love and concern for us. When we are tempted to dwell on the times that God has not answered our prayers the way we wanted them answered, we should remember the admonition in Philippians 4:8, where we are charged to think about things that are true, honest, just, pure, lovely, of good report, virtuous, and praiseworthy. We should dwell on these things, not on the negatives. Dwell on the expressions of love when God has delivered you, not on the times He did not come through when you wanted Him to do so.

I can remember times when God did not help me in the way that I wanted to be helped. There have been times when I could not figure out why God did not answer my prayer just as I had asked Him to. But then I recall later times when I understood why He did not answer my request exactly as it was made. There was the time that I had been away from my family for a month, and my heart ached to see them. I had been preaching in Los Angeles. I had a two-day gap in my schedule. I decided to hurry home to see my loved ones during the time off. I planned to catch a plane home as soon as I finished my last speaking engagement, and return in two days. Seldom have I been in such a hurry to get to an airport. I do not remember a time when I had more anxiety and a greater sense of urgency and panic about catching a plane. I nearly broke my neck getting to the airport, then rushed frantically through the airport terminal, muttering prayers and reassurances to myself, only to arrive at the departure gate as the plane was pulling away. I was heartsick. I thought of my sweet family, and I could see the disappointment in each face. I felt desolate as I plodded back through the terminal to leave, for there was no other plane home that night. I found a hotel room and spent a miserable night there. I felt that God had let me down. I wondered why He had not come through for me.

I went to breakfast the next morning, with plenty of time on my hands. I bought a newspaper and looked with horror at the headlines. The airplane I had missed by minutes had collided with another airliner in the high-altitude darkness of the night, over the Grand Canyon. It was one of the worst air disasters in history. I could only thank God for not answering my prayer to get me to the plane on time!

God Has Already Revealed His Purpose to Us

Paul, writing under the inspiration of the Holy Spirit, said that "all things work together for good" to those of us who love God (Rom. 8:28). That is good news!

But there is more in this verse than many people realize. We need to consider this passage in context. Let us look at some of the fine points of this revelation. The verse says, "And we know that all things work together for good to them that love God, to them who are the called according to His purpose."

First, notice that "purpose" is singular, not plural. God has only one purpose. And what is that? The passage goes on to say, "For whom He did foreknow, He did also predestinate to be conformed to the image of His Son, that He might be the firstborn among many brethren."

The purpose of all things working together for good, then, is clear. All things work together for good to conform all God's children to the image of Jesus. God wants all His children to be like Jesus! How many children could you love and take care of? Two? Four? Six? Eight? God's love is boundless. Unlike us, He can never have too many children. Unlike us, He is able to care for billions of children, without taxing Himself one bit. God has the means to care for all His creation. Imagine having billions of offspring and being able to lavish love on all of them. Few of us today can imagine what it must have been like for our great-grandparents to take care of a dozen or so children. Just imagine what resources it takes for God to care for billions!

How does one become conformed to the image of God's Son? Michelangelo removed all the stone that encased the "David" by chipping away all the marble which surrounded that beautiful form. God is in the process of hammering the chisel blows against the stone of our human nature. The hammer is difficulty and the chisel is trial. God sees in each of us that which is beautiful, much as Michelangelo saw David in that rough piece of marble. God is working away to create us to be the persons He wants us to be.

Let's take a "for instance." Suppose you are racially prejudiced. This, we know, displeases God. But, for this exercise, let's pretend that you are prejudiced. Then suppose that before long, an "undesirable" person moves in next door. With a great deal of effort, you manage to relocate to another house. After you are settled in your new home, another "undesirable" moves in next door. And so it goes: again and again, you move to get away from people of another race. But in time some of the people you thought were undesirable become some of the best friends you have ever had. They treat you with love and respect and you come to appreciate their friendship. In this case, God has taken you, a rough stone, and with hammer blows, the chisel has knocked off the undesirable part of you and brought out the beauty that was there all along. In the process, you have lost your prejudice.

Or suppose that you trust your bank balance and your stock portfolio for your security. You worry and fret and scheme to provide for your financial support. God may well have to bankrupt you so that you will learn to trust Him and not your bank balance for your security.

You may have to end up broke and bankrupt before you realize that your security resides with God and not on Wall Street. Sometimes God places us in pressure situations to help us grow. Sometimes He lets us bankrupt ourselves so that, broke and alone, we learn to trust Him as our eternal hope and security.

How much pressure does it take to get you on your knees before God? Do you remember the story of Jesus and the rich young ruler? Jesus told that young man he could find peace by selling everything he had and giving it all to the poor. The man went away sad because he had so much and was unwilling to give it away. Then there is another story about Zaccheus, who satisfied the Lord when he offered half of what he had to others. How far ahead of God is your money? Where do you place your priority?

Remember Always that God's Grace Is Sufficient

Now call to mind what His purpose is in the midst of your difficulty and trial. Then remember that in the midst of your problem, God's grace is sufficient to take you through whatever you have to endure.

How can you prove that God's grace is sufficient? How can you ever learn the treasures of His providence and the power available to you, if you never learn to depend totally and exclusively upon Him? How can this ever be known and experienced if you never encounter any problems, never go through any fiery trials?

In 1 Corinthians 10:13, we see the words, "There hath no temptation taken you but such as is common to man." Scratch the word "temptation" and replace it with the word "trial," a better translation. Now read the passage again: "There hath no trial taken you but such as is common to man; but God is faithful, who will not suffer [allow] you to be tempted [tested] above that ye are able; but will, with the trial, also make a way to escape, that ye may be able to bear it."

Many of us are tempted to read these words and say, "They sound so beautiful, but they just don't reflect what I am going through. No one has problems like mine!" This response is wrong, absolutely wrong. The Scripture makes it clear that what each of us is going through is no more—and no less—than what others have experienced. There is a difference in the specific circumstances and intensity that surround each of our problems, but we should not think that others are exempted from the problems we are experiencing. Others either are, have, or will experience heartache, personal loss, frustration, anxiety, jealousy, bitterness, fear, and all the other things that make this life different from paradise.

One of the biggest mistakes we Christians make is to assume that we are the only ones suffering some particular problem. We sometimes think that we are suffering because God is angry with us or that we are being punished and that other good Christians are not enduring the same events we are experiencing. When we feel this way, we need to stop and look around us. Just in our own Sunday School class, our prayer group, our church pew, we will find others experiencing heartaches, pain, and frustration similar to ours. Their specifics may be different, but their feelings are the same.

In 1 Corinthians 10:13 we are told that God will not let us be tested beyond our ability to endure the test. We all, no doubt, feel that there is a breaking point beyond which we cannot handle our frustrations and problems. Often we are tempted to say, "I can't stand it anymore!" That may be correct. We all have our breaking points beyond which we cannot go. We may not know exactly where that point is, but God does. He knows precisely how much we can take. Sometimes He likes to surprise us by taking us beyond what we think we can endure and handle. He gives us the grace to bear whatever the devil can put in array against us.

God provides us with a way to escape our frustration and anxiety. Again, 1 Corinthians 10:13 says, God "will with the temptation also make a way to escape, that ye may be able to bear it." Let me suggest that the Shakespearean English loses the heart of the Greek meaning for modern Americans in this particular verse. The combination of the words for "escape" and "to bear" in Greek give the idea of "being empowered to drive through the test." It is like a world champion football team driving through the opposing line to victory at the goal. The notion of running away from the test, of retreating, of shrinking from the heat, of fleeing with our tails between our legs, is totally foreign to the concept illustrated in the original language. God will not let you fail because He has tested your mettle before He put you in the fire. An old saying has it: "Only the finest steel has to go through the hottest fire." The trial makes us strong, and God is behind it all.

Focus on God's Ways, Not on His Acts

In our first point, we said that we should focus our attention on God's love, not on how many times He answered our requests exactly as we made them.

God has said, "My thoughts are not your thoughts, neither are your ways My ways" (Isa. 55:8). Truly, God's ways are far beyond us and many of His doings are mysteries to us. The Bible teaches us that God's ways and His thoughts are redemptive. They have their purposes and unfold for the good.

In contrast, when we focus on the acts of God, or on the acts that God has permitted, we become baffled that evil still holds sway in God's universe. The execution of His Son, the beatings, imprisonment, and martyrdom of His children all trouble us. These were terrible acts. And we wonder why God permits such things to happen. When Christians suffer, we ask, "Why?" When bad things happen to Christians, we ask, "Why?"

So why *do* these things happen? The answer is simple. God lets these things happen so that He might not violate the jealously guarded freedom of man's will, of man's right to reject God. God permits bad things to happen to Christians and others because He has given us our freedom, and part of that freedom includes the right to experience life as it is—good and bad, warts and all. God also permits these things to happen so that His righteousness might be known and so that mankind might learn to love Him freely, without coercion. Without life's experiences, we might be tempted only to trust ourselves. By facing the limits of our freedom, we realize our dependency on God.

The acts of God, or those acts which He permits to occur, should be considered separately from God's ways. God's ways are to operate within the acts of misfortune and evil to bring good out of them. Jesus was crucified, but through that act we are redeemed. Paul was imprisoned but behind bars found the time and inspiration to write several epistles. The list of examples of how God uses misfortune to bring good out of evil fills the Scriptures. They are illustrations of how God is continually outflanking mankind's rejection of Him to offer men and women repeated opportunities of salvation and to bring out the image of His Son in His children. At some time, in some way, in the acts God permits, you will see His ways or be assured they are operating for the good.

Never Forget the Nature of God

Instead of responding to our circumstances, we need to respond to the fact that God is God. We need to focus our attention on the nature of God, not on what He does or does not let happen in our lives. We need to delight in who He is. If our spirituality depends on our experiences, we are going to live on a roller coaster because the acts that God permits in our lives change. Perhaps one good way to understand this point is to remember that God loves us personally and is capable of spending time taking care of us, training us, and perfecting us. As we grow, God's acts toward us grow and change. The more mature we become as Christians, the better we understand the challenges God places before us.

God Promises Us a Better Tomorrow

In looking again at Romans 8:28, we must be careful to glean the exact meaning from its words. The text says, "All things *work together* for good," not that all things *are* good. Try sampling the individual ingredients of a chocolate cake the next time you make one. How does each ingredient taste? How about the raw egg? The salt? The baking soda? The bittersweet chocolate? Each ingredient is not too good by itself. Yet when they are all combined together and baked in an oven, all those bitter, sour, salty things have a way of combining together to produce a wonderful new taste. This is the way God acts in our lives. Many of the ingredients that go into making our lives are, by themselves, bitter, unhappy, and unpleasant. But combined together with and heated by the love of God, something wonderful is produced. Just as we look forward to what various kitchen ingredients can produce together, we should look forward with excitement to what God will make out of the disjointed, unharmonious factors in our lives.

How do we harmonize Romans 8:28 with the things in our lives that do not work out for the good? The answer: through the promise of God's tomorrow. There is no time reference in Romans 8:28. It says only that things do finally work out to the good. This can mean now, or in a few days, or in eternity. However it happens, God is faithful to His Word.

The best illustration of the point that we should live on the strength of God's promise of tomorrow is found in Hebrews 11, sometimes called "faith's hall of fame." We are reminded of Abraham, Isaac, Jacob, Moses, and others whose faith in God's promises sustained them even when they did not see the promised rewards in their lifetimes. Their confidence that God had spoken truly was all they needed to sustain their lives of faith and dedication. Yet we are in a better position to believe in God's faithfulness than they were. We have seen one of His greatest promises fulfilled: Christ has come.

All things *will* work out in God's time. The God who spoke the universe into existence has said so. I cannot promise that your problems will be solved any time soon or if ever; some things just will not change. There will be situations from which you will not be rescued. But consider why! And take heart because of tomorrow in paradise. Ours is a faithful God.

Faithful Because He Is Adequate

There is another side to the belief that all things work together for good. Paul expressed this attitude, which we referred to earlier: "I can do all things through Christ which strengtheneth me" (Phil. 4:13). Not only do "all things" work together for good, but we are also told that we can accomplish "all things" through Jesus Christ. God is at work in our lives even when we do not realize it, but He also works in our lives when we call on Him to help us.

Though these two biblical concepts may seem at first contradictory, they are actually two sides of the same coin. To Christians who trust and obey Him, God does work all things together for good, and Christ does strengthen them to do more than they could do on their own.

For the last few pages we have been writing about how God is faithful when He doesn't answer our every whim. Now let's focus on the fact that God is also faithful when He does give us strength to handle today and tomorrow.

When We Are Dreamers

I am a dreamer. I always have a project or a goal on the side that I am trying to accomplish. Often this is to the consternation of my family and my associates. There is a part of me that simply wants to retire to the country with a little house and a little church and a white picket fence. But, weighed in the balance, I am a dream-chaser, so I simply would not be happy with such an existence for very long.

Dream-chasers are always working on a "big deal." They are always going for broke, daring the impossible or the improbable. Such people cause grief for their families who would prefer predictability, stability, and security. But you know, we are all to some degree dream-chasers and that is good.

The Seabees, the construction arm of the U.S. Navy, have a motto, "Can do!" I want to say to you that through Christ you can do whatever is in your heart to do. Christ is not in the business of discouraging your basic nature to be an achiever. He is in the business of fulfilling that nature! Through Christ, you can do it! Whatever it is. Do not quit. You are not a cut-out paper doll just like the others in the row. God has made you the way you are, and if He has put greatness in your heart, achieve it through the power of Christ.

There are three ingredients that go into the achievement of that "impossible dream." They are, "I can," "I must," and "I will."

The "I Can"

Accept this: there is nothing you cannot do! "I can do it!" was the attitude of Thomas Edison whose impossible dream was to invent a light machine. Everyone tried to discourage him, to convince him to get a regular job and stop tinkering around with useless inventions. He had patented 1,093 inventions before he finally came up with the incandescent light bulb. One day, before he had made the discovery, he came out of his laboratory with a glow of enthusiasm on his face. His assistant exclaimed, "I see by your face that you have been successful!"

Edison replied, "No, but I found 79 more ways it cannot be done!" He was another day closer to the goal he knew he would reach—he did not doubt it.

The things that people have done! Some have memorized the entire Old and New Testaments of the Bible. Others have mastered more than 100 languages. A few have fallen thousands of feet without a parachute and lived. And some have broken the four-minute mile. The list of what people have done because of their impossible dreams is astonishing.

The four-minute mile is a good case in point of how, when people are convinced something *can* be done, they can do it. Once Roger Bannister finally broke this barrier, others began to do it. We see that it is often a psychological impediment that keeps us from achieving things. If you do not believe you can do something, you cannot. But those who believe that they can are like the people to whom the cup is always half full, not half empty. They are the kind of people who wake up and say, "Good morning, Lord!" instead of "Good Lord, morning!"

You say, "I can't do it." Yes, you can. You have surely heard the story of a man who fell into an open grave at night. It had been raining and he had taken a shortcut home through the cemetery. In the dark he stumbled over a mound of dirt and fell headlong into a freshly dug grave. It was deep and the drizzling rain had made the mud so slick that he could not get out. After trying and yelling himself hoarse, he finally gave up to wait until dawn. It so happened that another man, several hours later, took the same path through the graveyard and he too fell into the grave. He struggled frantically to get out but only succeeded in waking the man at the other end of the grave. As the first man, mud-covered and hoarse, woke up, he said to the man who had just fallen in, "It's no use. You can't get out of here!" But he did!

The "I Must!"

Are you convinced? Do you have the right attitude? Once you have the right attitude, you must also have the right determination.

I can, therefore, I must. When an impossible dream becomes possible in your mind, there comes a holy sense of "must," an "I've got to do it" attitude, a compulsion to do it. When your mind is set on achievement, powerful forces begin to focus in your mind to bring the thing about.

Most people aim at nothing and achieve their goal easily. But if we have definite goals, there is an imperative, a compulsion, to achieve them. My son has a poster on his wall of a skier flying off a high cliff, soaring above the snow with his body arched into the wind. It depicts an awesome exhilaration, a sense of having pressed beyond human limitations into a majestic, nearly superhuman venture. The caption reads: "You'll never know if you can until you try."

That caption is like the Christian faith. But Christianity is not something untested or unknown. The inconceivable potentials of Christianity have been tested throughout the ages. The realization of these potentials, however, can only come after a commitment is made to Jesus Christ. "I can do all things through Christ which strengtheneth me." I can, and therefore I must! Life will pay you what you demand of it. If you have concluded that you can and have followed that conclusion with the conviction that you must, there is yet another step to take.

The "I Will!"

I must, therefore I will. If you are relying on the Lord, you have the potential, the capacity, the power resident within you to do exactly what you want. God has given you the power of choice; and life will be what you make of it. A philosopher, who was said to be able to answer any question, was challenged by a young man who held a bird behind his back and asked him, "Is the bird alive or dead?"

The philosopher, knowing either answer would cause the young man to take action to prove him wrong, answered, "It is as you will, my son."

The decision rested with the young man, not with the philosopher. If the philosopher said the bird was alive, the young man could quickly and secretly crush the life from the bird. If the philosopher said the bird was dead, the young man could set it free, unharmed. It is the same with us humans. God has committed to us the freedom of choice. He has placed at our disposal power to achieve what He has given us to conceive.

There is a difference between failure and defeat. Failure is permanent; you can become a failure by not trying. But defeat is temporary—you try; you are defeated; but you can try again and again until you win. It is not the circumstances but your response to the circumstances that makes the difference.

During World War II, Germany demanded that England surrender. In the face of imminent destruction Winston Churchill, speaking for the British, responded that his country would fight on the land, on the sea, and in the air to the last drop of blood. He added that people would say later that this was their finest hour! Historians credit the resistance and survival of England largely to Churchill's response, which roused the British and gave them a will to fight.

If we must, we indeed must do something tangible; we must make a beginning. Some old-time preachers used to ask people to put their cigarettes and whiskey bottles on the altar as an expression of tangible action. An invitation given at the conclusion of a sermon offers people the chance to do something tangible. Christ told His disciples to do things—tangible things.

Businessmen tell me that the peril of middle management is the fear of failure. Many people in this strata of the business world never attempt anything for fear they will make a mistake and ruin their careers. Failure is not wrong, but failure to try is wrong. If we refuse to try, we refuse to win. We deny ourselves all sorts of possibilities.

Look at Peter. He tried. When he walked across the water to Jesus, the others sat in the boat; he sank into the water, but he went down trying. Remember the Parable of the Talents? (Matt. 25:14-30) Two men invested, risking their master's talents, and gained for him; another hid the talent for fear of failure and was pronounced a failure by his boss. Compare Paul's life. He fought a good fight (2 Tim. 4:7). He dared. He risked all and gave it all. And in so doing, Paul provided a drive and a direction for the young Christian church.

The fact that we can place our hope in an unchanging, faithful God gives us the assurance to fight the impossible fight, to reach for the unreachable star. We can do all things through Christ, because God is faithful to His Word.

The famous mountaineer, Sir Edmund Hillary, was lost from view as a few people watched him approach the summit of Mt. Everest. He was enveloped in a dreadful snowstorm. After an all-night vigil, the anxious newsmen were at their telescopes at first light looking for Hillary, but all they saw was the impenetrable whiteness of swirling snow and ice. The world listened impatiently as the report went out from the reporters: "Hillary last seen reaching for the peak!"

May it be said of us, "He (or she) was last seen reaching for the peak!" May it be said of us that we tested the resources of God and found Him faithful to strengthen us as well as meet our every need—even when we didn't understand His responses fully!